ROBBEN ISL

DEDICATION

For Matthew, Leila and Stephen who liberate me with their love;
and for those who risked their lives to free us all from the prison of apartheid

ROBBEN ISLAND

Charlene Smith

MAYIBUYE CENTRE

Mayibuye History
and Literature
Series No. 76

MAYIBUYE
BOOKS—UWC

ACKNOWLEDGEMENTS

This book could not have been written without the patience of, and endless cups of tea from, my son Matthew Smith; without the encouragement of a good friend and comrade, Barry Feinberg; without former Robben Island inmates opening up their hearts to me; without Tokyo and Judy Sexwale combing through their personal photographic collection and carefully captioning those pictures I selected despite their very busy schedule; without the patient support of those I worked with at Struik; and, most of all, without the inspiration of a wonderful country and the remarkable people who inhabit it.

First published by Struik Publishers
(a division of New Holland Publishing (South Africa) (Pty) Ltd)

New Holland Publishing is a member of Johnnic Communications Ltd

Cornelis Struik House,
80 McKenzie Street
Cape Town, South Africa
www.struik.co.za

Garfield House
86-88 Edgware Road
London W2 2EA
www.newhollandpublishers.com

Unit 1
66 Gibbes Street, Chatswood
NSW 2067, Australia

218 Lake Road
Northcote
Auckland, New Zealand

First edition published in 1997

ISBN 978 1 86872 062 0
10 9

Copyright © 1997 in published edition: Struik Publishers
Copyright © 1997 in text: Charlene Smith
Copyright © 1997 in map: Struik Publishers
Copyright © 1997 in photographs: as credited on each page
Photograph of Charlene Smith on back flap of cover © Robert Tshabalala

Managing editor Annlerie van Rooyen
Editor Alfred LeMaitre
Design manager & cover design Janice Evans
Designer & Cartographer Desireé Oosterberg
Design assistant Lellyn Creamer
Picture researcher Carmen Swanepoel
Project Coordinator Glynne Newlands
Proofreader & indexer Sandie Vahl

Reproduction by Hirt & Carter (Cape) (Pty) Ltd
Printed and bound by Paarl Print, Oosterland Street, Paarl, South Africa

*Front cover: Robben Island aerial (A. Proust); lighthouse (S. Adey/IOA). **Back cover:** Leper hospital (SA Library); Prison courtyard (UWC/Robben Island Museum/Mayibuye Archives); Nelson Mandela revisits the limestone quarry (The Argus). **Spine:** African penguin (E. Thiel/IOA). **Front flap:** Xhosa chiefs (SA Library). **Back flap:** Prisoner's letter (collection Charlene Smith).*

www.imagesofafrica.co.za
IMAGES OF AFRICA
PHOTO LIBRARY

CONTENTS

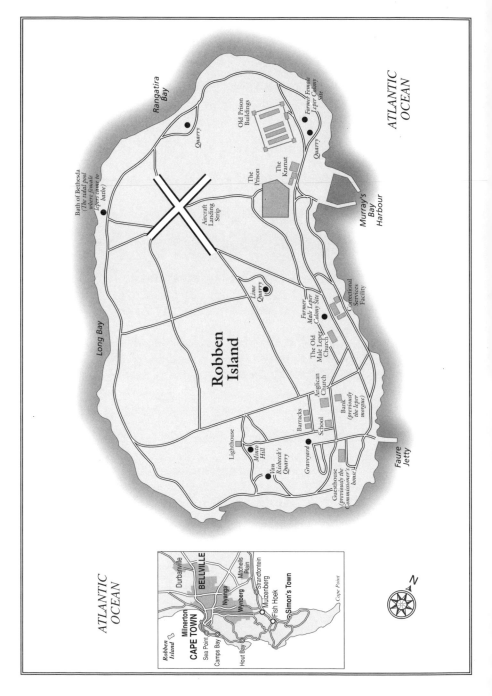

INTRODUCTION

Who can be unmoved on first hearing of its inhabitants – the
Lawbreakers, the Lunatics and the Lepers! Few places so small
and insignificant looking can boast of having played so
important a part in the history of a vast multitude of people.
I make no apology, therefore, for calling the attention of the
reading public to the Island's early history, I claim for it more
than a momentary passing attention; I call for respectful
and reverential regard.

'THE EARLY HISTORY OF ROBBEN ISLAND' BY G.F. GRESLEY,
CAPE ILLUSTRATED MAGAZINE, 1895.

In its small, wave-beaten boundaries Robben Island holds the memories of a nation and the legends of the greatest and weakest of South Africans. The Island has been the subject of books, poems, plays and a vast oral mythology. Better known as 'Esiquithini' (the Island) to the three generations of political prisoners who occupied it in the second half of the 20th century, it carries the scars of four centuries of human suffering and triumph. Its 12-kilometre circumference is like a small heart cut from the mainland bosom that for years monitored and regulated the pulse of a nation.

For most of Nelson Mandela's 27 years in jail, he lived on the Island. It was his suffering that made Robben Island a household word and a symbol of apartheid evil. He says now that had he been by himself he would have impressed no-one, 'but I was in the company of highly developed human beings. We spoke with each other about our problems and these discussions gave us self-confidence and uplifted us spiritually, freeing us from the negative obsessional side of life in prison.' And perhaps that shared experience, the learning, the knowledge that all are ultimately co-dependent and negotiation is more fruitful than conflict, honed wisdom and led to the evolution of South Africa's greatest sons.

The Island is 11 kilometres from Cape Town across a bitterly cold sea that snaps at the hulls of ships. Thick islands of kelp bob in the waters close to the shale beaches, and crayfish, lobster and perlemoen drift in its small inlets. It is a sea that arouses the conqueror in many, and usually delivers failure. Since at least the turn of the 19th century, swimmers have tried to beat the cold and the tides; in 1909 and 1926 it was women who managed to make the swim across the bay without the benefit of wetsuits. On May 11, 1993, University

SOUTH AFRICAN LIBRARY: ATTRIBUTED TO DR WANGERMANN

Impressionistic linocut, 1868, showing Xhosa chiefs imprisoned on Robben Island, with the few buildings then on the Island.

of Cape Town student Alan Langman managed the 7,2-kilometre swim to Bloubergstrand in two hours and 40 minutes.

These swimming feats probably mean that Robben Island may have had more succesful escapes than its jailers have cared to admit. Did, as an example, 20-year-old Jan Kamfer, the only recorded escapee in the 20th century, die in the icy waters after he stole a paddleski from outside a warder's house on March 8, 1985, and paddled furiously to the low, beckoning finger of Bloubergstrand?

He could not have chosen more perfect conditions. The Port Captain's office said the wind in Table Bay at the time of the escape was south-easterly and the swells small. It was possible for a person on a paddleski to make it to the mainland.

A massive sea and air manhunt was launched after Kamfer failed to respond at evening roll call and a paddleski was discovered to be missing. On March 11, prison officials said Kamfer had certainly drowned, after all, they had found no trace of him. They pointed out that the sea around the Island is infested with sharks and the water, they claimed, cold enough to kill a man in 45 minutes (a claim which early 20th-century swimming conquests proved fallacious).

Sergeant Koos Vrey, who worked on the Island when Kamfer escaped, said the paddleski had a hole in it. He doesn't believe Kamfer's escape was succesful, and even if the paddleski remained afloat, he said, 'at that time there were three large sharks we often saw around the Island; one was a shark of about 5,5 metres'.

Maybe Kamfer, like Langman, showed nothing is impossible with skill and a strong will. But that is not always enough; Xhosa prophet Nxele Makana and 30 fellow prisoners were less fortunate. They drowned during an escape

---

Victorian visitors to Robben Island were ferried on a steamer called Tiger *and carried to the shore from rowboats by prison labourers.*

'Tiger' Conveying passengers

At the Bazaar — Making Purchases.

Returning home — Farewell to our Visitors

Mode of Landing at the Island.

attempt in 1820, after a small boat they had stolen from whaler John Murray capsized close to Bloubergstrand. Africanists among the political prisoners of the 1960s to the 1990s called the island Makana Island and claim his ghost walks the Island still.

A ROCKY OUTPOST

Robben Island is flat, and one is surprised that monstrous waves have not reclaimed it. At its highest point it is 30 metres above sea level and receives only 300 millimetres of rain a year. The underlying rock is blue slate of the Malmesbury Series, covered by blown coastal sands and a dusting of limestone. Generations of bleached, crushed shells make the white Island sand glisten with an almost unbearable sheen. When Nelson Mandela underwent cataract surgery in July 1994, surgeon Percy Amoils said the operation was complicated by the fact that his tear ducts were corroded by years of exposure to limestone dust from his labours in the quarry.

Roads on the Island are made either of dirt or of stone chiselled by political prisoners in the quarries and then tarred. Scattered across the Island are wattle, bluegum, pine, cypress, tamarisk, manitoku and acacia trees, none of which are indigenous. Most trees were imported by seafarers, and were planted between 1892 and 1912. The remaining natural veld was destroyed to make way for fortifications during the Second World War.

Bartholomeu Dias was possibly the first mariner to land at Robben Island, in 1488. His second-in-command, Joao del Infanto, was, according to historical records, the first white man to set foot on the Island. Other Portuguese followed in 1502, some living in a large cave which they named Portugal. For aeons before the arrival of Europeans, however, the Khoi and their antecendents had ferried back and forth from the mainland to the Island.

Joris van Spilbergen named it Isla de Cornelia after his mother, in 1601. He left two dassies on the Island that his crew had removed from Dassen Island. The dassies thrived and formed the basis of an important meat supply for later generations of seamen. Most mariners referred to the Island as either penguin, seal or Robben Island. In 1611, Jacob le Maire and some sailors were left on the Island by le Maire's father, Isaac, to club seals for pelts and hunt whales for their blubber. As many as 4 005 seal skins were exported to Europe from the Island during the early 17th century.

Sir Thomas Herbert, the English explorer, first raised the idea of a victualling station in the Cape. As a consequence, in 1614, at the special request of the English East India Company, 10 convicts were sent to establish a settlement. Little interest was shown in the island after this debacle, other than as a place where seafarers left messages and notes to each other under rocks, or alighted to harvest dassies, seals or the fat-tailed sheep bartered from the Khoi and left to multiply on the Island. But the British had sketched the Island's destiny as a place of banishment. In March 1636, Hendrik Brouwer, former governor-general of the Dutch East Indies, banished to Robben Island the ringleaders of an attempted mutiny.

Sixteen years later, ship's surgeon Jan van Riebeeck succesfully colonised the Cape for the Dutch East India Company. The Island became a larder for the early colonists, a place where they could hunt animals and birds, collect eggs, grow crops and fatten livestock. But the colonists quickly denuded the Island of its natural wealth. In 1654, Van Riebeeck issued South Africa's first conservation decree, banning the further slaughter of the dwindling colonies of sea birds.

Settlers used stone from the Island for building material. Its shells were crushed and burnt in a kiln erected in 1654 to produce lime, used for paint and plaster. These were the first industries of the colonial Cape. The first cornerstones of the Castle were cut on Robben Island, and were laid by Governor Zacharias Wagnaar on January 22, 1666. Slaves hewed stone and lime from the Island while soldiers did the building.

But Van Riebeeck confirmed the Island's role as a place of banishment when he exiled his wily interpreter Autshumao (or Herry) there in 1658,

---

A group of lepers dressed in their Christmas best late in the 19th century. Lepers were resident on the Island until 1931.

together with two other Khoi, Simon Boubou and Khamy or Van Cou. The Dutch valued the Island as the British had, because it was difficult to escape from and because it concealed dreadful conditions.

Some years later Herry's beautiful niece, Krotoa (or Eva), who grew up as a favoured maidservant in the Van Riebeeck household from the age of 10, married the Dutch surgeon and explorer Pieter van Meerhof on June 2, 1664. The wedding was a lavish celebration befitting a favoured child; she was 21, he 27. (A mere 20 years later, however, under Governor Simon van der Stel – a

By 1872, the Island was a busy community with more than 1 000 inhabitants. The rock in the left corner of the picture is Whale Rock upon which many a ship has foundered.

Racist attitudes did not begin with apartheid. The attitudes represented by those who set up this photograph plagued South Africa from the earliest times of colonial settlement.

Mauritian Creole – marriage between whites and freed slaves of 'full colour' was prohibited, although whites could marry 'half-breeds if they chose', but by then tragedy had already visited the Van Meerhof couple.)

The couple moved to the Island a year later, when Van Meerhof became its superintendent. Their predecessors were Jan Zacharias and his Bengali wife. Van Meerhof had special instructions to rid the Island of vipers, snakes and spiders, but was killed during a visit to Madagascar two years later. A bereft Eva returned to the mainland with her three children. The devastated widow began drinking and sleeping around; once she was found naked, smoking a pipe on a beach. On another occasion she abandoned her children at the Pottery House to live at a Khoi encampment. She was found and banished to Robben Island – the first of many occasions – before she died at the age of 31. Her children grew up with foster parents in Mauritius, and two of them later returned to the Cape. Her son died shortly after his return but her daughter married a wealthy farmer called Piet Zaaiman.

This beautiful painting of the Anglican church on Robben Island was completed by a mental patient at the turn of the 19th century.

The Kramat on Robben Island, just outside the prison walls, is a sacred site for Muslim pilgrimage and celebration.

A PLACE OF PUNISHMENT

By this time Robben Island was a convict station and farm. In 1673 it gave pasturage to 880 oxen, 313 cows, 3 457 sheep and some pigs. The animals fared better than the prisoners. In 1671, five Khoi prisoners were sent to the Island, after being flogged and branded, for stealing sheep. Three were sentenced to 15 years and two to 17 years, but managed to escape not long after. The following year, Thuintjie van Warden, wife of a burgher, was found guilty of 'evil-speaking' against other women and 'was sentenced to retract the slander, ask forgiveness, be bound to a post for one hour, and then suffer banishment for six weeks to Robben Island'.

The theft of vegetables was one of the worst offences. Two soldiers found guilty of stealing a few vegetables in 1672 were flogged and sent to work in irons for four months. Three years later two slaves who stole vegetables had their ears cut off and were sent in chains to Robben Island for life. J. Jans, a freeman, caused a scandal at the Cape when it was revealed that he had picked the pockets of a drunk, and regularly intoxicated his dogs and pigs by feeding them a mixture of eggs, sugar and wine. His property was confiscated, he was flogged and sent to work in chains on the Island for three years.

In the eyes of the colony, though, sodomy was the worst crime of all. For this offence, Rijkhaart Jacobsz of Rotterdam and Class Blank, a Khoi, were thrown into the sea with weights tied to them between Robben Island and the mainland on August 19, 1735. The Island thus became entrenched as a symbol of the denial of human and political rights.

From 1681, the Dutch brought political prisoners from Malaysia, India, Ceylon (Sri Lanka) and Indonesia to the Cape. These prisoners were either incarcerated on the Island or forced into slavery. They were fed the same mixture of seal and penguin meat mixed with seaweed that the pigs thrived on. While some were treated with unspeakable cruelty, others brought their wives and entourages and received stipends from the Dutch.

In 1738, Regent Doumano of Termanos was banished to the Cape for being 'dangerous' and a 'disturber of the peace', and four minor kings were incarcerated for life with him. In 1747, the Dutch rulers in Indonesia sent Said Alowi of Mocha, a Muslim priest, into exile on Robben Island where he spent 11 years before being moved to Cape Town to work for the Chief of Police. The following year, Dain Mangenan, a Macassar prince, joined the Indonesian royalty on the Island. In 1769, Eugenius Monoppo, King of Boelong and Mongodo, was sent to Robben Island as a prisoner of state for two decades, with an allowance of 36 rix dollars a year. In 1788, when Achmet, Prince of Ternate, who was jailed for running a brothel, was released from banishment he returned to Indonesia with his wife, her mother and grandmother, four children and servants.

In 1969, a kramat was erected on Robben Island over the grave of Sayed Adurohman Moturu, the Prince of Madura, who died on Robben Island in 1754. A political refugee who ministered to the Malaysian slaves before being banished to the Island, it was said he could materialise through closed doors to slaves who needed his help. After his death, his family exhumed his remains and took them back to his homeland. The shrine became a place of homage for departing political prisoners, from the 1960s to the 1990s, who would bow before it when leaving the Island. It is also visited by descendants of Malay slaves each Sunday. Every February, a feast – the Khalifa – is held here.

FROM PRISON TO LEPER COLONY

In 1833, Captain Richard Wolfe took over as commandant of the penal settlement, bringing with him artist Thomas Bowler, his children's tutor. In 1841, Wolfe built the first church for the village. Originally Anglican, it is now multi-denominational. A cream structure with turrets, it resembles an ornament from a wedding cake. Fifty-four years later, the simple stone Church of the Good Shepherd, also an Anglican church, was designed by Sir Herbert Baker and built by lepers. It was a men-only church, and had no pews because most lepers could only lie or stand.

In 1844, John Montagu, secretary to the government, decided the prisoners could be put to better use building harbours and roads on the mainland. In their place he had lepers removed from Hemel-en-Aarde near Caledon to Robben Island. The Island became the dumping ground for the unwanted, the desperately ill, the blind, the impoverished, the insane and the criminal.

Montagu believed hard work calmed male lunatics (as they were called) so they were put to work in the Robben Island quarries, returning at night to cells. Lepers slept in the military stables or erected small tin shanties, but this led to complaints from prison authorities about promiscuity. The island oozed misery. Conditions were abysmal. Into this morass of pitiful humanity, Sir George Grey banished the proudest – and in his view, the most treacherous – of the Xhosa chiefs after the Eighth Frontier War (1850-53). He could have humiliated them in no more powerful way. More than a century later, some of their royal descendants were imprisoned here, too.

Word filtered into the colony in the late 19th century about the bad conditions on the Island. Between 1852 and 1909 a dozen commissions investigated conditions on the Island. The infirmary was condemned and patients removed to the mainland. In 1890, female paupers were sent to Grahamstown, and in 1913 the mentally ill were relocated.

By 1892, there were 1 070 people living on the Island. They celebrated their semi-permament status two years later by building the first primary school, which in 1993 had four teachers and 50 pupils. A magnificent guest house was built to serve as home to the Island's commissioner, and two years later Faure Pier was erected, complete with a tramline from the top of the pier to the village. Lepers remained on the Island until they were relocated to Pretoria in 1931. James Fish, a missionary who worked with the lepers for 34 years from 1889, wrote of meeting 25 lepers on the docks in April 1915. They were cured and had been sent back to the mainland. One man had been on the Island for 45 years. 'Poor things,' he wrote in his diary, 'it must have been almost like life from the dead to be released.' The leper church and a vast cemetery with rotting wooden crosses bear witness to this sad period in the Island's history. After the departure of the lepers, the Island's only inhabitants for a decade were the lighthouse keeper and his family.

And then came the Second World War. By 1940, naval technicians were hard at work converting the Island into a fortress. Murray's Bay harbour and an airfield were constructed and gun emplacements built. After the war, the

South African Navy took it over as a facility for training seamen: The SAS Robben Island flourished until it was handed to the Department of Prisons in 1960. The maximum security prison was completed by 1964.

In 1993, Ahmed Kathrada, who was interned on the Island with Mandela, said: 'Someone has written about two prisoners looking out of their cell window: one saw iron bars while the other saw stars. The real picture of prison life is one of great warmth, fellowship, friendship, humour and laughter, of strong convictions, of a generosity of spirit, of compassion, solidarity and care. It is a picture of continuous learning, of getting to know and live with your fellow beings – but more importantly where one comes to know oneself, one's weaknesses, inadequacies and potential. By reducing prison life to cold, impersonal statistics one is blotting out the deep, multi-dimensional experiences, feelings and interests of a vibrant community. We would want Robben Island not to be a monument to our hardship and suffering but a triumph of the human spirit against the forces of evil. One cannot divorce the Island's history from the nonpolitical side ... there is the flora and fauna, the architecture and the shipwrecks around the Island.' The following chapters examine the multifaceted legacy of a banishment that consistently failed to vanquish the human spirit.

A doctor attends to a patient in the female 'whites only' ward at the Robben Island leper infirmary, March 1904.

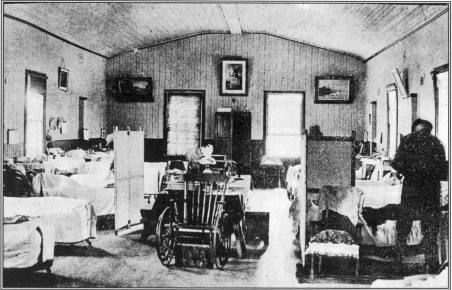

ENVIRONMENTAL ASSETS

The following is a list of what we once succeeded in catching in five hours – 11 Galjoen, 42 Hottentots, 32 Stumpnose, 16 Klipfish, 58 Mossbankers, 7 Jacobpeevers and a couple of impertinent sharks, who would persist in putting in their noses where they were not at all wanted. Total 171.
WJR, ROBBEN ISLAND TIMES, DECEMBER 25, 1886.

Over the centuries, sailors and settlers transformed Robben Island from a windswept island with a few storm-battered shrubs and a brackish, barely palatable water supply, into a larder and a gentleman's hunting preserve. Today, the Island is an important nature reserve, and the home of a number of endangered species.

The explorer Le Vaillant wrote in 1790 that the Island took 'its name from the marine dogs (seals) found there'. He also saw political prisoners: 'The unhappy exiles each day deliver a certain quantity of limestone which they dig; they fish or cultivate their small gardens which procures the tobacco and other indulgences. It is astonishing to see how large vegetables grow; cauliflowers are of an amazing bigness; their goodness exceeds their size. There are likewise violet coloured figs of exquisite smell. The wells furnish water as good as that at the Cape, an extraordinary phenomenon in an island of such small extent and almost level with the sea.

'I saw a great number of serpents of four to five feet long, but they are not dangerous. Partridges and quails are found here in abundance, I sometimes shot from fifty to sixty of a morning.'

Little wonder then that the Island's postmaster, who also edited *The Robben Island Times* each week from 1884 to 1886, wrote on December 20, 1886: 'Owing to the reckless destruction of our feathered game last year by self-invited sportsmen, it has been found absolutely necessary to refuse all permits to shoot partridges or pheasants during 1887. No guns or sporting dogs will be allowed on the Island.' He somewhat petulantly went on to declare: 'the number of applicants desirous of slaying our rabbits and quail and trenching on our good nature and hospitality is yearly on the increase and to avoid giving offence the Surgeon Superintendent (who governed the isle) thinks it imperative to revive this rule as otherwise, everything in the place will be shot down and preservation of game rendered impossible.'

Some of the worst devastation to fauna and flora, both indigenous and imported – such as pheasants and fallow deer – had occurred long before this,

The seas around the Island are known for their bounty. Here warders (from left) J Boyce, Sgt Carroll (police officer), M Luder, B Luder and J Barber display a catch of snoek.

however. Only two years after the arrival of Dutch settlers at the Cape in 1654, Jan van Riebeeck became aware of the threat to the colony's food reserves, and issued SA's first environmental edict — that the slaughter of sea birds and penguins should cease.

Because of its isolation from marauding Khoi, who for two centuries attempted to repel foreign incursions at the Cape, the Island had become a kind of pantry for settlers and seafarers. The African penguins (*Sphenicus demersus*) on the Island had been an important source of fresh protein to seafarers since at least 1497, when sailors of the Portuguese ship *Saldanha* reported feasting on seals, penguins and tortoises harvested on the island after a mainland skirmish with the Khoi. In 1647, after the Dutch ship *Haarlem* foundered, the crew survived by feeding on sea birds and penguin eggs until rescued. The Dutch settlers under Van Riebeeck would follow their example.

The first men from Van Riebeeck's colonising party sailed to the Island on the *Goede Hoop* in September 1652, five months after settling on the mainland. Captain Sijman Turner and his men returned to the Cape settlement with 100 cormorants, some penguins, 3 000 sea bird eggs and a number of live seal pups. In his journals, Van Riebeeck noted some time later that gulls destroyed eggs left in the nests that had been disturbed by the crew of the *Goede Hoop*. But the colonists needed fresh protein, and Khoi clansmen and mountains barred easy access to the wildlife of the hinterland, so the Island soon became the focus of regular food gathering expeditions. In May 1653, Van Riebeeck supplemented the Island's small herds of hardy cattle and sheep, apparently first left by Dutch Admiral Maaklof in 1608 as a ready larder. The sheep in particular flourished, despite the brackish water. For their Christmas roasts in December 1657, colonial cooks were able to select from a flock of some 400 plump sheep.

To supplement food stocks and give diversity to supply, Van Riebeeck brought rabbits and dassies from Dassen Island in April 1658. However, the dassies ate the eggs of nesting birds, or the birds themselves. Together with the threat from the indigenous mole snakes, the changed conditions led to flocks of birds leaving the Island to nest in safer coves.

By this time, seals had also begun to leave the Island, where they had bred for centuries. The seals have still not returned in breeding colonies. Many swam further up the west coast to Saldanha Bay were there were, and still are, vast breeding colonies. A year after Van Riebeeck settled at the Cape, a French ship that had been moored near Saldanha Bay for six months sent word that it was returning to Europe with 48 000 seal skins and a hold filled with barrels of seal oil.

But, as Le Vaillant wrote, penguins were also an important source of oil: 'The government sends every year a detachment to the Isle of Roben to shoot

In August, when grey rain clouds begin parting to allow a bolder sun, Robben Island flings off its dull winter coat and is filled with fields of white lilies, chinchirees and Namaqualand daisies to pay homage to the warmer months that lie ahead.

mors and manchets, which are called at the Cape, penguins, from whom they extract great quantities of oil.' In 1777, adventurer Edward Terry expressed the opinion that Robben Island was also named Penguin Island, probably by a Welshman – in Welsh, penguin signifies 'white head'. With the white sands of the island flecked with the bobbing white heads of penguins it is a credible explanation. Researchers from the Sea Fisheries Research Institute in Cape Town – Bruce Dyer, Rob Crawford, H. Boonstra and Leisha Upfold – believe there were more than a million African penguins at the start of the 20th century, but by the mid-1980s only 160 000 were left worldwide. Human intrusions saw populations falter as their eggs were harvested and their guano collected, while fishing boats plundered the seas of the pelagic fish the penguins survive on. While the African penguin is listed in the Red Data Book as 'vulnerable' to extinction, from Dassen Island northwards along the Atlantic coast of Africa the bird is endangered. The breeding grounds of Robben Island are vital if this species is to continue.

As shoals of anchovy and sardines diminished through overfishing, so did the numbers of sea birds. Seals, too, forced birds out of traditional breeding areas. On some important sea bird breeding islands, such as Possession Island off Namibia, wildlife protection rangers are employed solely to monitor the breeding patterns of birds and to whip any seals that intrude onto the island back into the sea in search of other breeding grounds. Young bull seals, which conservationists say are the worst ravagers of bird nesting areas, are shot if they kill birds.

On Robben Island birds are carefully observed and tagged. Nests and breeding sites, birds and chicks are counted. The African penguin is monogamous, retaining the same breeding partner for life, and like salmon they return to the same shores to breed each year. The peak mating season for penguins coincides with an annual abundance of anchovy off the west coast from April to September. Young birds, usually aged between a year and 22 months, sleek after their December moult, dive and compete with their parents and other birds. Careful marine conservation measures over the last two to three decades have seen increases in shoals of anchovy and sardines and, with them, the return of more sea birds.

In 1978, the elegant bank cormorant (*Phalacrocorax neglectus*) returned to Robben Island, after an absence of generations of humankind, and built nests on the northern breakwater of Murray's Bay. Breeding flocks of the crowned cormorant (*P. coronatus*), Hartlaub's gull (*Larus hartlaubii*) and swift tern (*Sterna bergii*) have also returned. In March, 1991, the Island became one of 28 new sites adopted by the SA Natural Heritage programme because of its importance as a sea bird breeding colony. A number of rare and endangered birds nest on the island, including listed Red Data species such as the Damara tern, Caspian tern, black eagle and African penguin. The northern portion of the Island, where most birds breed, is a protected reserve. The birds dive not only for fish, but for tiny plankton called diatoms which dust the dark seas like icing sugar and wash in foamy mounds on beaches where the sun dries it into a springy white carpet. African prisoners used to call it 'the white scum from the sea', and hack it from its accumulation on rocks and in the quarries.

Also in search of the diatoms come whales. The beautiful southern right whale and other whale species can be seen close to the shoreline, where some calve. Sergeant Wayne Cook, a public relations officer on the Island during its final prison days, recalled with awe seeing a huge whale close to shore: 'A large school of dolphins circled her and one in particular raced around her spinning out of the water in thrilling leaps. Suddenly the whale lifted her head clear of the water, and as if she was curtseying after ballet bowed back under the waves and raised her tail as a baby whale was born.' He said the dolphins which had protected her from the great white sharks and other predators that frequent the seas around the Island went into a frenzy of delight, leaping through the waters to herald this new sea child. 'It was,' Cook recalled, 'the most graceful sight I have ever seen.'

A NATURAL SANCTUARY

The Island is becoming a monument to preservation, and after the August rains it rewards those who protect it with a blanket of white arum lilies and Namaqualand daisies. Beautiful black oystercatchers, with their red beaks, red legs and red ringed eyes pounce on oyster and abalone (*perlemoen*) on the rocks. Long black mole snakes bask on the hot, glittering white sands – the residue of millenia of crushed shells – or slither to the huge sea bird nesting colonies and daintily swallow eggs or fledglings.

The West Coast Rock Lobster Sanctuary envelops the Island, and government approval is needed to harvest lobster or abalone in these waters. Despite this, the waters around the Robben Island have long been favoured by night-time poachers, who not only harvest crayfish and abalone but also plunder the wealth of marine archaeological artefacts that remain in the seas around the Island. Most of the abalone taken by poachers is dried and sent to the Far East, while lobster finds its way onto gourmet tables in Johannesburg or wedding banquets in Tokyo.

In the past, prison warders seem to have supplemented their income through this lucrative and illegal trade. Former political prisoner Saths Cooper said warders would bring bagfuls of abalone for prisoners to clean, presumably for resale on the mainland. The prisoners would always steal a few and roast

them over the blacksmith's coals. Former Rivonia trialist and longtime Robben
Island political prisoner, Wilton Mkwayi, said they would pick up *perlemoen*
while collecting the seaweed the prison exported to the Far East, and boil it
over wood fires at hidden braziers around the seashore. 'We knew all the best
places to get *perlemoen*. Not even the Cape-born prisoners knew this. One day
one said, "man I really want *perlemoen*, how do you get it?" We said "move
your foot," he was standing on one. He thought they were stones. We took a
spoon to dig out the flesh, it was delicious.' Mussels were also favoured and
were grilled on zinc sheets over small fires.

But fish stocks around the Island are still poor. Desiree van Zyl, from 1972
the Island storekeeper for more than 20 years, said in their early years her husband would sometimes come home from a morning's fishing with 200 snoek.
'By 1993, he was lucky to catch two a weekend.'

Robben Island's natural island vegetation is a drier version of strandveld,
with a few reeds and gentle froths of erica shrubs. Today, conservationists are
trying to eradicate foreign vegetation. Since 1985, the bluegum trees planted
as camouflage for gunnery emplacements during the Second World War have
been felled because of their high consumption of precious ground water. Sixty-
two percent of island trees were imported more than a century ago and blue-
gums have thrived.

Small herds of eland, springbok, bontebok, duiker, ostrich and steenbok
brought to the island in the last century graze within snuffling distance of
squawking sea birds or drink from the rainwater reservoir at the south side of
the Island. Around 35 fallow deer, brought by Victorian settlers, hide in the
underbrush away from modern conservationists, who are culling them with the
aim of ensuring South Africa's indigenous creatures only on an island that his-
torically was little more than an arid wasteland.

BIRDS

Bokmakierie (*Telophorus zeylonus*)
Bulbul, Cape (*Pycnonotus capensis*)
Chat, familiar (*Cercomela familiaris*)
Cisticola, fantailed (zitting) (*Cisticola juncidis*)
Cisticola, greybacked (*Cisticola subruficapillus*)
Curlew, Eurasian (*Numenius arquata*)
Dikkop, spotted (*Burhinus capensis*)
Dikkop, water (*Burhinus vermiculatus*)
Dove, Cape turtle (*Streptopelia capicola*)
Dove, laughing (palm)
   (*Streptopelia senegalensis*)
Dove, Namaqa (*Oena capensis*)
Duck, yellowbilled (*Anas undulata*)
Eagle, black (*Aquila verreauxii*)
Egret, cattle (*Bubulcus ibis*)
Egret, little (*Egretta intermedia*)
Flycatcher, fiscal (*Sigelus silens*)
Francolin, Cape (*Francolinus capensis*)
Francolin, greywing (*Francolinus africanus*)
Greenshank, common (*Tringa nebularia*)
Guineafowl, helmeted (*Numide meleagris*)
Gull, kelp (*Larus dominicanus*)
Heron, blackcrowned night
   (*Nycticorax nycticorax*)
Heron, blackheaded (*Ardea melanocephala*)
Heron, grey (*Ardea cinerea*)
Hoopoe (*Upupa africana*)
Knot, red (*Calidris canutus*)
Moorhen (*Gallinula choloropus*)
Mousebird, whitebacked (*Colius colius*)
Nightjar, fierynecked (*Caprimulgus pectoralis*)
Ostrich (*Struthio camelus*)
Oystercatcher, African black
   (*Haematopus moqini*)
Partridge, chukar (*Alectoris chukar*)

Peacock (*Pavo cristatus*)
Penguin, African (*Phalacrocorax coronatus*)
Pigeon, speckled (*Columba guinea*)
Plover, blacksmith (*Vanellus armatus*)
Plover, common ringed (*Charadrius hiaticula*)
Plover, crowned (*Vanellus coronatus*)
Plover, grey (blackbellied) (*Pluvialis squatarola*)
Plover, Kittlitz's (*Charadrius pecuarius*)
Plover, threebanded (*Charadrius tricollaris*)
Plover, whitefronted (*Charadrius marginatus*)
Robin, Cape (*Cossypha caffra*)
Sanderling (*Calidris alba*)
Sandpiper, common (*Actitis hypoleucos*)
Sandpiper, curlew (*Calidris ferruginea*)
Shrike, fiscal (*Lanius collaris*)
Sparrow, Cape (*Passer melanurus*)
Sparrow, house (*Passer domesticus*)
Starling (*Sturnus vulgaris*)
Starling, redwinged (*Onychognathus morio*)
Sunbird, lesser doublecollared
   (*Nectarinia chalybea*)
Sunbird, malachite (*Nectarinia famosa*)
Swift, African black (*Apus barbatus*)
Swift, little (*Apus affinis*)
Teal, Cape (*Anas capensis*)
Tern, Arctic (*Sterna paradisaea*)
Tern, caspian (*Hydroprogne caspia*)
Tern, common (*Sterna hirundo*)
Tern, damara (*Sterna balaenarum*)
Tern, sandwich (*Sterna sandvicensis*)
Tern, swift (*Sterna bergii*)
Turnstone, ruddy (*Arenaria interpres*)
Wagtail, Cape (*Motacilla capensis*)
Weaver, Cape (*Ploceus capensis*)
White-eye, Cape (*Zosterops pallidus*)

Source: SA Department of Sea Fisheries

MARITIME HISTORY

'So the whale called down his own throat to the shipwrecked
Mariner, "Come out and behave yourself. I've got the hiccoughs."'
RUDYARD KIPLING, 'JUST SO STORIES', 1902.

At the turn of the 19th century, while aboard a ship sailing past Robben Island, the writer Rudyard Kipling was regaling passengers with a story, when a large 'sea monster' rammed the vessel and became entangled with the propellors. The ghost of a Malay fisherman, who is said to arise from the waves warning of peril, had not emerged from the topaz bay to alert the skipper, nor had the captain seen the phantom of a black hound with burning red eyes bark a warning from the narrow white beaches of the Island. No warnings came, even though there are phantoms aplenty around the Cape of Good Hope. The most famous of these – the *Flying Dutchman*, its sails in tatters and mast creaking dangerously – had not been seen in decades.

The passengers of the *Armadale Castle* would no doubt have loved to sit wrapped in the sharp aroma of smelling salts while all these phenomena appeared to amuse them, but even the sea monster was a blessing from the boredom of the long sea journey from England. They dashed to the railings and gazed upon a marine creature some 9 metres long, its poor body thrashing as it tried to escape. Finally the ship's engines were reversed and with blood staining the water purple the 'sea monster' sank beneath the waves. The Victorians loved tales of sea monsters, and many sightings were made in the 19th century and the early 20th century around Robben Island and Table Bay. In thick mists curling around a weak torch or ship lights, strange creatures readily rise.

One rainy, winter's night in July 1975, with fog so thick it was difficult to see more than a few metres ahead, aliens landed on Robben Island, or so a warder on night patrol around the Island perimeter radioed back to base. Magdalena Cillie, who was serving as the Island switchboard operator, took the call from the terrified man: 'He said he had seen strange creatures walking along the road.' A detachment of burly, well-armed prison officers went to investigate and found a group of soaking, exhausted Taiwanese seamen, their clothes torn, oil streaking their bodies, struggling through a wind that threatened to cast them back into a sea that had crushed their ship. The shipwrecked sailors of the *Fong Chung No. 11*, a Taiwanese tunny boat, were brought to the officers' mess, where they were fed hot soup and sandwiches, given warm blankets and dry clothes. Once the angry seas died, the castaways were ferried back to the mainland.

SOUTH AFRICAN LIBRARY

Issie, *a hardy ferry named afer the wife of former South African Prime Minister,*
General Jan Smuts, ploughed the seas between Cape Town and the Island for many years.

Others have lived to tell the tale, but none in a more convivial way than
those who survived the sinking of the *Bernicia*, which was on its way out of
Cape Town harbour in June 1861, well stocked with fine Cape wines and
brandies. Barely out of port, heavy winds and seas threw the vessel against
Whale Rock, the large Robben Island sentinel that has claimed many a ship.
The captain herded some passengers and crew onto a lifeboat. Four sailors
were tossed overboard as the ship bucked in the swell, and the men grabbed
onto brandy casks before being flung onto the shores of Robben Island.

While the captain and other survivors bobbed by in the pouring rain and
bitter cold, the sailors did what any sensible shipwreck survivor clinging to a
barrel of brandy would do: they cracked open the casks and drank deeply to
steady their nerves and bring a little warmth to their shivering bodies. It was
not long, however, before this tonic had worked so well that they began a
Bacchanalian revel on the beach. They were soon joined by some curious lepers and mentally ill who, hearing the commotion, came to investigate. An
almighty party ensued but, alas, one mental patient imbibed more alcohol than
his system could accommodate and died the next day.

DUCATS AND PHANTOMS

The seas around Robben Island have enough tales to forever delight a Kipling. For many years pirates plagued the Cape route and become part of Cape shipping lore. Not all the tales of pirates and sailors have survived, but the ocean still deposits clues for the sharp-eyed beach ambler. Walking along the stony beaches or jagged rocks of Robben Island one may still find a heavily encrusted gold ducat, a piece of sealing wax from parchment that has long since disintegrated, or a fragment of porcelain that travelled from China or Japan in the 17th or 18th centuries before being claimed by Neptune.

One of the sea's great ghost stories takes place around the Cape: Van der Decken, otherwise known as Bernard Fokke, was a rude, loud ship's captain who sailed the Cape route for the Dutch East India Company early in the 17th century. In 1641, as his schooner reached the Cape, the wind changed and huge waves curled over the ship. Robben Island was nearby and the dark Cape mountains just visible above the high waves. The passengers and crew begged to be put ashore on the Island but Van der Decken, drunk with arrack and half mad with the tedium of voyaging, swore at them and kept to the wheel.

And then, legend tells us, a cloud appeared and from it a shaft of light poured onto the deck carrying a celestial figure. The terrified crew and passengers sank to their knees, but Van der Decken drew his pistol and shot at the figure, who cursed Van der Decken to sail the seas forever with no port or harbour, only gall to drink and hot iron to chew. The being disappeared, taking the passengers and crew, but forgot a hapless cabin boy, who was left with the demented captain. Sailors said the ship had curious low bows and a large, lit lantern astern. They warned that any ship that went close would see its captain go mad and the boat overturn.

There have been a number of recorded sightings of the *Flying Dutchman*. In 1750, a terrified Cape fisherman said he had seen it. A warship, the *Leven*, spotted it off Orange Point in 1823. English sailors swore they saw the ghostly apparition in 1835 and, 20 years later, the crew of a French ship sighted it. The last known sighting was in 1881 by the men of the *Bacchante*.

The *Flying Dutchman* was probably helped in his ruthless quest by Robben Island's Whale Rock, which only reveals its sleek back in calm weather. At other times, the rock disappears under the waves and, without a Lorelei, awaits the hulls of poorly navigated passing ships.

Whale Rock is helped, in turn, by the foul temperament of the Cape of Good Hope, where the weather makes the clouds over Table Mountain furl and unfurl like a fussy housekeeper adjusting a table cloth to get the creases perfect. They lose their wispiness and suddenly thicken, becoming as dark and angry as the visage of a bully. The sea, too, changes from an intensely beautiful, almost translucent aquamarine to a gentle dove grey and then to a deep, terrible slate that threatens to pull anything under. The sun, taking fright, rapidly retreats to the placid climes of the Karoo while the waves rise and clap against each other and the rocks.

WRECKS

Early in 1648, a Dutch East India Company vessel arrived at the Cape with surgeon Jan Anton van Riebeeck aboard. It was his task to curb the debilitating and usually lethal scurvy that afflicted seamen travelling that route. On his return he suggested to the Dutch East India Company's Council of Seventeen that a station be established at the Cape to provide fresh vegetables, meat and water to ships sailing to the spice ports of India, Malacca and Madagascar. He volunteered his services, and arrived in Table Bay with three small ships, the *Dromedaris*, the *Goede Hoop* and the *Reiger*, on April 6, 1652.

Shipping increased around the Cape and wrecks began to accumulate in the bay. In 1657, Van Riebeeck established the first navigation facility on the Island's highest point – Fire Hill, now known as Minto Hill – 30 metres above sea level. The flag of the Prince of Orange was raised and huge bonfires lit at night to warn approaching Company ships of the jagged rocks that flank the Island. In 1863, the present lighthouse was built to replace fire beacons. The lighthouse is 18 metres high and had a light of 464 000 candlepower. In 1938, the lighthouse was converted to electricity, giving it a beam that can be seen from 25 kilometres away. After the loss of the *Tantallon Castle* in 1901, the first of a number of foghorns were built. These were replaced by an electrical warning system in 1980.

Over the centuries at least 29 ships — many with valuable cargo – have been wrecked off Robben Island. The earliest recorded wreck was that of a Cape-built yacht, the *Schaapenjacht II*, on August 15, 1660. On that day, Cape burghers saw a signal fire on Robben Island. The next day they sent over a boat and discovered the *Schaapenjacht II* had been beached, and was in fine condition but for a gash on the side. Van Riebeeck ordered that it be dismantled and a fresh keel laid for a new sloop called *'t Vliegertjen*, renamed the *Musquitjen* not long after. The *Musquitjen* became one of a sucession of small craft dedicated to ferrying people and goods between the mainland and the Island.

In 1655, Van Riebeeck sent men to cut trees to build the *Robbejacht* (Seal Hunter), a 17-ton yacht with a crew of six men. As its first task, the vessel took bricks to Robben Island for the building of a milk cellar.

Two years later, the *Voerman* was built by Cape carpenters at Groote Schuur. A hard-working little sloop, it took part in cattle-bartering expeditions as far along the coast as St Francis Bay. But most of its work consisted of the dull routine of ferrying casks of salt to Robben Island and returning with up to 60 sheep a time.

The *Bruydegom*, launched in November 1663 in Table Bay, ferried slabs of blue slate quarried from Robben Island for the stoeps, kitchen floors and grave covers of the colonists. The little boat served the Company well, even helping to foil an escape attempt when Robben Island prisoners hijacked it in 1665. The *Bruydegom* finally went aground at Hoetjies Bay on April 9, 1674 and was dismantled, its seaworthy planks used to build another small sloop.

The *Bruydegom's* boards may have been weakened by worms – the constant peril of Cape shipping. Two years previously, a plague of worms saw the Cape almost devoid of seaworthy craft. No lime or stone could be brought from Robben Island for the extensive building operations taking place at the colony. Only a small vessel, the *Oyster*, remained free of this scourge and did what it could to ferry supplies.

Ships from all the great shipping nations of Europe – Holland, France, England and even Scandinavia – stopped to fetch sheep, seals or penguin eggs from Robben Island and fresh produce from the colony when they rounded the Cape. The little wooden ships fought the seas to Malacca and India for spices, to Japan and China for fine porcelain and pottery, and to the Indonesian archipelago for woods, spices and the cowrie shells so vital for bartering in the slave trade. The East India Company sold cowries to the West India Company to barter with West African communities for slaves. The first slaves at the Cape, three men and eight women, were brought from West Africa in 1657. As Dutch imperialism spread and Oriental resistance grew, slaves were brought from Malaysia, Indonesia and Sri Lanka. Cowries were also used in Asia as money tokens. Wrecks found in Table Bay often have cowrie shells littered around them or encrusted by barnacles onto porcelain. Cowrie shells are also rumoured to be on board the most coveted of the 3 000 wrecks that litter South African waters – the *Dageraad*, which sank off Robben Island in January 1659. It was one of 246 losses incurred by the Dutch East India Company's fleet of 1 772 ships, of which 52 now rest in South African territorial waters. Of these, 18 were lost in Table Bay alone.

The three masted, 140-ton *Dageraad* was built in 1692 and went down two years later in heavy mist and an unseasonal north-westerly wind off the west coast of Robben Island. Among the survivors was a sailor called Suliman, whose guardian angel must have been working overtime: he had survived another shipwreck shortly before, that of the *Gouden Buys*. The *Dageraad* was one of three ships that salvaged treasure and other goods from the *Gouden Buys*. Seventeen chests of gold went down with the *Dageraad* and only three were recovered.

The *Gouden Buys* sailed from Enkhuizen in Holland with 190 passengers on May 4, 1693. By the time it dropped anchor off St Helena five months later, most of those on board were desperately ill with scurvy. On November 11, seven men left the ship to find help. Five perished. Suliman was found by Khoi who took him to the fort at Saldanha Bay. Suliman's shipmate was found after seven weeks of aimless roaming.

Suliman said that sailors from the *Dageraad* went aboard the beached *Gouden Buys* and heard Jan Frans Doeburg, the chief steward from Amsterdam, pleading deliriously: 'Don't kill me I will tell you where the money is.' He was taken aboard the *Dageraad* but died two days later. The crew of the *Dageraad* and those of its two accompanying vessels salvaged all they could before the sea broke up the *Gouden Buys*.

On its return to the Cape, the *Dageraad* sailed into Table Bay during a perfect night with a light mist painting gauze across the stars. Then the wind changed, smashing the *Dageraad* against a reef. Suliman was washed overboard and scrambled onto the shore of the Island. Splinters of wood were washed ashore but 17 chests of gold coins disappeared below the waves.

In 1728 two English divers made unsuccesful attempts to salvage items from the wreck, but were hampered by temperamental weather. Since then, islanders have on occasion found a few gold ducats and silver pieces of eight in rocky pools. In August 1944, soldiers of the wartime garrison were digging tunnels near the lighthouse when they found a skeleton and a number of French silver and copper coins bearing dates from 1688 to 1726.

MARINE ARCHAEOLOGY

Pioneering research into the marine archaeology around the Island has been undertaken by Professor Bruno Werz of the University of Cape Town. In 1990, he was involved in a project called Operation Sea Eagle that mapped 24 wrecks, positively identifying 22 around Robben Island. It was a difficult task, with six-metre waves and strong undercurrents making diving perilous. Most shipwreck material was found close to the shore at depths of less than 10 metres, with most artefacts wedged between rocks or in gulleys.

Werz and Navy divers scoured nine square nautical miles around the Island, but the use of normal detection equipment, such as side-scan sonar, a proton-magnetometer and even underwater metal detectors, was severely hampered by the wild seas. Metal buoys attached to sites with steel cables were often washed away by the tides.

Werz's studies indicate that fog, darkness and heavy rainfall were the main causes of shipwrecks around the island. Poor visibility led to the wrecks of the

The British steam liner, Rangatira, ran aground off Robben Island on 31 March 1916. Over the centuries, at least 29 ships have been wrecked off the Island.

Bernicia, Gondolier, Tantallon Castle and *Hypatia*. Dense fog was the cause of the foundering of the *Fong Chung No. 11, Rangatira* and *Golden Crown*. Thirteen of 21 disasters occurred between 9:00 p.m. and 5:30 a.m., when human fatigue may have played a role. The *C. de Eizaguirre*, which sank in 1917, probably struck a mine, and the *Forfarshire* came to grief in 1864 because the ship had no chart of Table Bay.

The most glamourous 20th-century wreck was that of the *Tantallon Castle*, a mail steamer which sank in dense fog in the early hours of May 7, 1901. The ship had left harbour with 120 passengers asleep in their cabins. Double lookouts were guiding it out of the bay when one reported seaweed, a sure indicator of proximity to Robben Island. Captain de la Cour Travers shouted, 'full astern!' but there was 'a thump, a thud and a slow grinding impact' as the *Tantallon Castle* shuddered along a reef.

Signal guns were fired from Robben Island. The master of the small coasting steamer *Magnet* pitched his deck cargo overboard and sent a whaleboat to the aid of the sinking vessel. Women and children clambered aboard. Harbour tugs arrived, together with the *Braemar Castle*, the *Avondale Castle*, the *Raglan Castle* and *HMS Tartar*, but the *Tantallon Castle* resisted efforts to tow her off the rocks. Not one life was lost before the great ship, lying broadside to the swell, broke up and disappeared.

Bruno Werz believes the marine history around the Island is so important it should be made into an archaeological reserve. Sitting in his office at the University of Cape Town, Dr Werz sits with his back to a view that stretches to the milky-blue Hottentots Holland Mountains. A battered pewter mug salvaged from a wreck lies on a table. Below it is a plastic bag filled with 500 grams of peppercorns – still in pristine condition after being locked for 300 years in the hold of the *Oosterland*, buried beneath silt in the icy waters of the Atlantic halfway between Robben Island and Paarden Eiland. In a bucket of water are little packets of pottery shards from the wreck of a Dutch East India Company trader which sank in 1697. The water serves to desalinate the pottery and enhance its preservation potential.

Werz lifts out a particular treasure, a grime-encrusted lice comb. 'Now this,' he triumphantly informs, 'is something you would never find at a land dig. We are going to have this comb analysed to get an idea of the sort of insects the ship's crew were infested with and to give us information on the level of hygiene on board ship.' The comb is carefully placed in a packet waiting for archeometrists to dissect it, germ by germ, to unravel the secrets of men who lived three centuries ago.

The *Oosterland* is the first archaeologically salvaged wreck off Africa. Most salvage operations around the South African coast have been carried out with no respect for the historical information that wrecks yield. Only three previous salvage operations – those of the *Sacramento* (1647), *Doddington* (1755) and *Birkenhead* (1852) – adequately recorded findings.

From the *Oosterland*, Werz and his team have recovered textiles, indigo, tropical woods and nuts, coconut shells, earthenware, porcelain and spices. They have found shoes, wicker baskets and wooden tools that would decay in land sites. There is spectacular porcelain that has caused museums from England to Japan to revise the dates of their collections. Items include whole and fragments of plates, bowls, large vases, incense burners, teapots, exquisite miniature vases, and figurines of eagles, ducks and lions.

The *Oosterland* was built in Middelburg, Holland, between 1684 and 1685. On its second voyage, in 1688, the ship brought a party of French Huguenots to the Cape, including the forebears of the De Klerk, Du Plessis, Nourtier (Naude) and Theron families. It left for its fourth and final voyage in the spring of 1694, with 342 people on board (111 of whom died on the voyage), and reached Indonesia on June 11, 1695.

On the return trip, the *Oosterland* finally arrived in Table Bay in May 1697, together with the *Zion*, *Waterman*, *Assendelft* and *Overrijp*. Many crew members were ill from drinking contaminated water, and while they recovered and awaited the rest of the fleet from Indonesia, weather conditions began to deteriorate. By May 23, strong north-westerly winds were blowing and the sea was choppy. The *Kattendijk*, which was part of the fleet, broke anchor early on May 24 and went adrift. It rammed the stern of the *Oosterland*, severing the anchor cable. More anchors were dropped to try and save the vessels. The *Kattendijk* was brought under control, but some hours later the *Oosterland* snapped its cables again, drifting into the shallows where it foundered. All aboard perished, except for four people who made it to shore. Two died the following day.

WRECKS

Ships that have foundered on or around Robben Island include:

Schaapejacht II, 15 August 1660
  (Cape-built yacht)
Dageraad, 20 January 1694 (Dutch)
Flora, 17 November 1821 (Dutch)
Perseverance, 12 March 1826 (British)
Gondolier, 7 February 1836 (British brig)
Bittern, 18 January 1848 (British brig)
Kingston, 23 December 1852 (US barque)
Sea Eagle, 16 November 1856 (US ship)
Timor, 22 December 1856 (Dutch barque)
Bernicia, 16 June 1861 (British barque)
A.H. Stevens, 7 February 1862 (US clipper)
Forfarshire, 15 September 1864 (British ship)
Il Nazareno, 2 December 1885 (Italian barque)
Tantallon Castle, 7 May 1901
  (British mail steamer)
Natal, 24 May 1914 (Norwegian steam whaler)
Rangatira, 31 March 1916 (British steam liner)
C. de Eizaguirre, 26 May 1917
  (Spanish mail steamer)

Golden Crown, 18 July 1923
  (British steam trawler)
Hypatia, 29 October 1929
  (British cargo steamer)
Solhagen, 11 September 1936
  (British steam whaler)
Erica, 1958
Rebecca, 1959
Rotterdam, 1970
Fong Chung No. 11, 4 July 1975
  (Taiwanese tuna fishing boat)
Goel No 1, 27 January 1976
  (Canadian oil research ship)
Pieter Faure
Daeyang Family, 30 March 1986 (Korean carrier)
Chanson de la Mer, 6 November 1986
  (South African yacht)
The Apollo Sea, July 1994 (Chinese ore carrier)
Hang Cheng II, April 1998
  (Taiwanese fishing trawler)
Sea Challenger, April 1998 (SA service vessel –
  trying to pull the *Hang Cheng II* off the rocks)

Sources: Robben Island Harbour Master; Bruno Werz, UCT; various historical research journals.

ESCAPES:
LOOKING FOR THE ROAD

*Kukazakulu Nxele (the coming of Nxele Makana,
the great Xhosa prophet).*
A XHOSA PROVERB THAT REFERS TO ANYTHING THAT IS LONG
EXPECTED BUT NEVER OCCURS.

There was an old coloured man, known only as Plaatjes, a mental patient on
Robben Island, who each day plodded the beaches searching for planks
from old wrecks to build a boat. He would sit at a spot where, if he looked up,
Cape Town would rest in his eyes. In his hands his hammer and saw would
mould the wood as if caressing the breasts of a beloved. He would be left to
his musings and his work until the boat took form and developed into a sea
voyager, then hospital attendants would splinter the vessel and burn the wood.

Plaatjes would watch impassively as his craft was carried across the sea by
ash and smoke. When it was little more than a pile of soft white embers

---

*Plaatjes, a mental patient on the Island, on an escape vessel he made. The twin superim-
posed on the photograph is an example of those he made from brass gleaned from beaches.*

unravelling before the wind, he would rise and head for the beaches and more wood and the brass for coins he would never use.

When there was not enough wood to build another boat he would collect the brass that he found while beachcombing. He would hammer it flat into coins on which he would carve a likeness of Queen Victoria. Someday, when his boat set sail, he would walk into the stores of Cape Town and pay with his own money. Someday.

Plaatjes died on the Island, but for many others escape became reality. The Island has enjoyed a reputuation as an impenetrable fortress, surrounded by a bitterly cold tempestuous sea and great man-eating sharks, from which few have succesfully escaped. But escapees have used boxes, rafts, animal-skin boats, hijacked schooners, paddle-skis and, if they had the skill, their own swimming power. There have been enough swimmers who have made the crossing without body-warming wetsuits to show that a strong body, determination and no hungry sharks may be all one needs to succeed in the bitterly cold waters.

In 1909, an unnamed swimmer made it from the Island to the mainland. Fifteen-year-old Peggy Duncan, a tall, stocky, 15-year-old in November 1926, swam the 'long route' – Robben Island to the Adderley Street Pier – in nine hours and 35 minutes. Even today Robben Island is a favourite venue for the Long Distance Swimmers Association, who hold relays from there to Bloubergstrand.

But most escapees used boats to make their getaways. Because of the abundance of seals and sheep on the Island, boats made from skin were favoured by escapees in the 18th and 19th centuries. In 1731, seven men put to sea in a small boat made of skins. Governor de la Fontaine ordered a commando to search the coast from Blaauwberg to Groenekloof, and four drenched fugitives were found. Their boat had capsized before reaching shore and three of their number had drowned.

On the evening of February 26, 1844, a tub was used by William Smith and James Hunt. However, soldiers of the 45th Regiment opened fire on them and Smith's body fell from the tub. Next day, a drenched and tired Hunt gave himself up. Boxes made a boat for five lepers who escaped from the Island in 1896; however, they too were recaptured when the boat capsized.

Carel and Jacob Kruger challenged the seas late in the 19th century in a boat made of animal hide, and succeeded in landing at Blaauwberg before hastening into the interior. Carel's freedom was short-lived: he disturbed an elephant who trampled him to death, and was buried in the Prieska district in a place still known as Carel's Graf. Jacob Kruger became a wild man of the interior for 20 years, and then was granted a free pardon to live the life of a slothful burgher. Admiral Stavorinus in 1789 described the life of Cape burghers as 'a very easy life. The men are seldom seen abroad: they are generally at home, in an undress, and spend their time smoking tobacco and loitering up and down the house. After dinner they play cards. They are not addicted to reading and are consequently very ignorant and know little of what is doing in other parts of the globe, except what they may hear from strangers who visit from time to time.' Fate removed such indolent options from Jacob Kruger: while travelling to Cape Town, a lion ate him.

THE ISLAND'S FIRST PRISONERS

The only prisoners to escape to the Island were a group of highwaymen under Captain James Cross, who were given the choice of the noose or life as the first settlers of the Cape. If British plans for the settlement of this group of murderous criminals had not been so badly botched, South Africa could have become like Australia – a land settled by convicts.

There are many variations on the tale of Captain Cross, a large bully of a man who served as a yeoman of the guard to King James I, but the most accurate version is probably that given by Edward Terry in 1777. Cross, being a man of foul temper with a ready sword, 'had his hand in blood twice or thrice by men slain by him in several duels'.

In 1614, he and nine others were convicted of heinous crimes at the Old Bailey in London. They had their execution stayed by the entreaty of the East India merchants, on condition that they be banished to the Cape, 'in the hope that they might discover something advantageous to trade'.

Two of the group never made it to the Cape. One, Duffield, was taken on as a servant by Sir Thomas Row – a foolish act because Duffield was no sooner employed than he stuffed his clothes and bag with Row's silver and ran away, never to be seen again. Another died on the journey. Eight men were deposited on shore with some ammunition and provisions, such as dry biscuits, hoes and turnip seed, and a small boat to carry them to and from the Island for eggs and penguin or seal meat to balance their diet.

They set up camp, and it was not long before the curious Khoi wandered down to meet them. Some bartering began, but Captain Cross soon became quarrelsome and began to abuse the Khoi. It was their land and they were disinclined to be hectored by this fat, red-faced stranger, so 'many of them got together and filled his body with darts and arrows'.

The other seven 'miserable banditti' did not need a second warning. They ran to their little boat and rowed to the Island. Whales were calving in the bay, however, and one rose as the miserable and terrified convicts rowed over her. Their boat split, and they were fortunate to make it ashore onto the desolate and barren shore. At that time there was not a tree on the Island. There was little fresh water. Birds and penguins filled every portion of shoreline area not occupied by bleating seals or slithering mole snakes. But sheep and dassies occupied the hinterland.

The men lived there for five or six months, through wild Cape squalls and with the harsh sun beating on their shadeless bodies. They grew half mad with terror, hunger and isolation. One day, just before sunset, they saw the white masts of a ship entering the bay. The last rays of the sun coloured the sails as gold as a chalice. Four of the desperate men put to sea in a raft, but the tide was against them and they were carried out to sea. Ghostly wails pierced the gathering gloom as the waves claimed their crude vessel and the men drowned.

The next day the ship sent a boat to the Island and rescued the other three. But it is a mark of the calibre of these men that history records they behaved so badly on board ship that they were frequently put in stocks. Within three hours of their return to England, they had stolen a purse and were soon executed by the now impatient British law.

The Cross group are the first known prisoners to have lived on the Island, and their misery was matched by others over the centuries. Escape became an imperative, matched by the illusion of embrace by a mainland that seems remarkably close. On good days, the sea is as placid as a pond. It is only when one is on the sea, halfway between shores, that one realises how far away land is and how deceptive is the sea's mirror surface.

A MIRROR OF THE TIMES

Punishments on the Island were a reflection of the harsh attitudes of mainland rulers. The Dutch traveller Stavorinus commented: 'Punishments are very severe here, especially with regard to Oriental slaves. In the year 1768, I saw one who had set a house on fire, broken alive on the wheel, after the flesh had been torn from his body in eight different places with red-hot pincers, without his giving any sign of pain during the execution of this barbarous sentence which lasted a full quarter hour. Impalement is in use here, as well as Batavia.'

Offences by women, particularly those who embarassed their husbands, were dealt with severely. A woman who committed adultery with the master woodcutter was divorced from her husband on August 9, 1708, and sentenced to five years imprisonment in Indonesia (Batavia) while the woodcutter was sentenced to two years on the Island.

Over the years a popular method of escape was to hijack a large vessel and sail it to other parts. Thirteen years after the establishment of the colony, a group of convicts attempted to steal the *Bruydegom*, which was used to

A leper's boat, built in secret, was discovered hidden under a mound of beach sand and destroyed before escape plans could come to fruition.

convey sheep and stone from the Island to the mainland, but this attemp was foiled. In 1716 and 1718, there were two succesful hijackings – a Chinese fishing boat and a British vessel, the latter with the aid of English sailors.

One of the most succesful hijacks took place on November 10, 1817. A military sentry and four convicts escaped from the Island in one of the whaling boats belonging to John Murray, a whaling contractor who worked from the Island. The men boarded the ship *Elizabeth*, which was lying just off Murray's Bay. The master of the ship later told the fiscal (chief of police) that a little before midnight he heard a commotion and went to the deck. Twelve people had boarded his vessel; one fired a musket at him, another cried that the ship was taken. He was locked in his cabin and guarded by two sentries. Coogan, a naval convict, was in charge of the hijackers and gave orders for the cable to be cut and the sail hoisted. The captain was ordered to hand over the keys to the ship's strongbox.

Coogan ordered that no-one was to be harmed. When the ship was safely out at sea, he lowered a longboat for his hostages, and gave them a bucket of water and seven loaves of bread. By 11 a.m., the *Elizabeth* was cutting a fine wake behind her as she sailed off in a north-north-west direction. The captain and his crew rowed furiously to Cape Town, and from there sent a message to the sloop *HMS Mosquito* at Simonstown, but the naval vessel was unable to stop the *Elizabeth* before it reached the high seas.

The most famous escape attempt in South African prison lore was that of the Xhosa prophet, Nxele Makana, who had led an abortive raid on Grahamstown in 1819. The same year, he was jailed on Robben Island, and within months attempted to escape. The plan appears to have been masterminded by two prisoners, John Smith and a man called Holmes. One morning, when a guard opened their cells about 30 men overpowered him, stealing his weapons and others from the barracks. Eight soldiers were wounded in the melee, but the prisoners had the advantage of surprise and numbers. They ran to John Murray's whaling operation, stole a longboat and headed for Blaauwberg beach. However, the boat rammed the rocks fringing Blaauwberg beach and most of the occupants were drowned. Legend has it that Makana clung to a rock shouting encouragement to his comrades before he drowned. Smith and two other escapees were caught and hanged, then decapitated and their heads fixed to stakes on the Island as a warning to others. After this episode, Murray was forced to close his whaling operation.

For the most part, the Island protected colonists from having a guilty conscience, particularly in the 19th century when the chronically ill – whether cancer patients, epileptics, diabetics or others – were abandoned there, along with the insane, lepers, criminals, the destitute and political prisoners.

John Montagu, a governor of the Cape, was scandalised by conditions on the Island during his visit in 1843. He informed the Colonial Office that there were 183 convicts on the Island, of whom 116 were coloured and 8 were white 'natives of the colony'; there were 59 Europeans, of whom 37 were soldiers. Prisoners were given rations of rice and bread but no vegetables; they had no cooking or eating utensils: 'They cook their victuals and eat them, when, where and how best they can. All this should be remedied.' There was a foul stench in the wards because some men had crude

Covered in a generous swathe of natural insulation, Florrie Berndt successfully swam from Robben Island to Cape Town in 1926.

SOUTH AFRICAN LIBRARY

cloth bags next to their beds in which they hung the meat of the animals slaughtered in hunts on the Island.

Montagu decried the fact that there was no educational instruction of convicts and that the medical officer lacked adequate supplies. He wrote that a budget of £25 a year was set aside for the Island administrators to buy sheepskins and bullocks' heads to make veldschoen for the convicts. 'One sheepskin and two bullocks faces make two pair at a cost of one shilling per pair,' Montagu reported. He suggested the establishment of a hospital and the provision of better clothing, and that petty offenders be put to work building roads for the colony while only the worst criminals would remain on the Island. Montagu transformed the Island into a place for a different type of social castaway: to Robben Island were moved lepers from Hemel en Aarde and Port Elizabeth, and the insane from Somerset Hospital in Cape Town. They were joined by paupers who had been housed at the SA College at the head of Government Gardens.

The plight of these people was pathetic. One mentally ill woman was a sturdy black woman who dressed in men's clothes and claimed she was an African king. A small man from St Helena who believed he was Jesus always carried a Bible which he claimed he had written. Those who disagreed with him were subject to violent tantrums.

Those prisoners who lacked the will or ability to build boats escaped in other ways. Island records are filled with accounts of people drowning in the ocean, the leper pool or the water reservoir; others hanged themselves or slit their throats.

May Harvey, a nurse who worked on the Island for a decade, walked into the bitterly cold sea on July 10, 1874. It was rumoured she was pregnant with an illegitimate child. Nonetheless, a plaque was erected in the church commemorating her death. Luke Quinn, an invalid, was recuperating in the home of Island resident Ralph Harvey. On August 9, 1848, a beautiful spring day, Harvey claimed he had gone to the well to fetch water and, on his return, found the house doors locked. Peering in a window, he saw Quinn with his throat slit, bleeding to death on Harvey's bed: what a fabulous tale probably rests under that bland description written by the Island scribe! Two months later, on October 18, Herman Titus beat to death an elderly fellow mentally ill patient, William Scott. A year later, Petrus Henrickse, who had been admitted to the 'lunatic asylum' six weeks previously, walked into the room of his terminally ill father-in-law, R. Jurgens, and without speaking a word picked up a knife, slit his own throat and walked back to his bed where he lay down and bled to death.

Escape attempts in the 20th century tended to be complicated and doomed. Jeff Masemola spent more years on the Island as a political prisoner in the 20th century than any other individual. Together with Sedick Isaacs, a teacher, Masemola devised a plot to escape. Masemola was also a teacher and master craftsmen in metal. There was little he could not fashion from the twisted bits of metal washed up on shore. He was kept in a single-cell block and allowed a small workshop and some tools, including a grinding stone.

Saths Cooper recalls that Masemola was 'somewhat paranoid and kept a large collection of knives, but behind all this was a perfect copy of the master key that could unlock all cells'. The plan was that he and Isaacs would sneak sufficient medicine from the dispensary to put in the wells and put the warders to sleep. They would then open the doors of the prison, put together a raft they had built and concealed and sail to Cape Town. Winter was the time to do this, they had decided, because the tides – although choppy – would carry them to Cape Town.

On the night before their plan was to be implemented, warders burst into Masemola's cell, pushed past him and went straight to the air vent where he had hidden the key. An *impimpi*, or informer – a fellow Pan Africanist – had revealed the plan. The men were whipped and had almost a year added to their sentences.

Eddie Daniels hatched a wild scheme in 1985 that, although it received careful consideration on the Island, was put into a pigeonhole by the ANC in exile. The plan was that on New Year's Day 1991, at 9:15 a.m., a helicopter would hover over the Island and drop a basket for Nelson Mandela and Walter Sisulu to escape in. The Island High Command under Mandela discussed this, and decided that the ANC had to leave a key figure on the Island. Accordingly, Sisulu would stay but SWAPO founder and leader, Andimba Herman Toivo ja Toivo, would accompany Mandela to a friendly embassy on the mainland, from where an additional escape plan would have to be devised.

In November 1989, when Daniels was released from prison he gave the sketch plan – stuck to a postcard carried by a friend, Moira Henderson – to Randolph Vigne, a former comrade in the African Resistance Movement. The postcard was given to Oliver Tambo, but fortunately nothing further was heard about the plan.

Rather than face Victorian gossip about her pregnancy, spinster May Harvey drowned herself – and won the Islanders' sympathy.

SACRED TO THE MEMORY OF
MAY HARVEY,
WHO WAS FOR TEN YEARS A FAITHFUL SERVANT
OF THE ROBBEN ISLAND INSTITUTION,
AND WHOSE DEATH BY DROWNING
ON THE 10TH DAY OF JULY 1894,
IS DEEPLY MOURNED BY HER FELLOW-WORKERS.

SO TEACH US TO NUMBER OUR DAYS, THAT
WE APPLY OUR HEARTS UNTO WISDOM.

MARK WIDDICOMBE

XHOSA CHIEFS

We have to have the courage to say that during the colonial period
sometimes we were colonised with the help of our own leaders, our
own chiefs and our own kings ...
SEMBENE OUSMANE, SENEGALESE WRITER AND FILM-MAKER.

I
t is one of history's ironies that little more than a century after the great
Xhosa chiefs were incarcerated on Robben Island, their heirs in the African
National Congress would begin their imprisonment a few metres from where
the Xhosa chiefs lived out their jail sentences in huts made with tarpaulins and
saplings. The stories of men such as Makana, Maqoma, Siyolo, Sandile and
others added a fresh chapter to the saga of the Island as a place of exile and
confinement. Thus, the story of the gradual destruction of the Xhosa nation at
the hands of colonialists is intimately linked with the story of the Island.

The story begins on the frontier of the old Cape Colony, in the attempts
by settlers and colonial authorities to gain control of African land. By 1817,
governor Lord Charles Somerset had arranged a system of 'passes' to allow the
amaXhosa to visit the fairs held twice a year at Grahamstown and Fort Wilshire
on the Keiskamma. By the 1820s this system was used to regulate Xhosa
labour. Missionary Charles Brownlee wrote in 1823, that Xhosa were being
'induced into the service of Boers with threats of Robben Island'.

The rule of law became a cloak to disguise blatant injustices. The Xhosa
chiefs erred in believing their oppressors were men of principle. They did not
initially oppose the entry of the colonists to the land. After all, the Xhosa had
also settled on these plains aeons before, after migrating from Central Africa.
They were not opposed to sharing the land. But the Cape colonists sent raiding parties to steal Xhosa and Khoi women and children as slaves. They took
Xhosa cattle to boost Cape herds. Instead of uniting against a common oppres-
sor, the Xhosa weakened their forces by continuing petty battles among themselves and relying on the disastrous prophecies of soothsayers and war doctors.

British Kaffraria, as the British called this vast territory, had lush hills and
verdant valleys. Rivers crisscrossed it, and the sea rolled onto shell-speckled
beaches. Shipwrecked sailors were occasionally found on the beaches, and were
taken in by Xhosa clans who cared for these strange, pale creatures from the
sea. Many castaways took Xhosa or Khoi wives and became part of the south
Nguni culture. One such white child, rescued as a castaway, grew up to marry
a Pondo chief and become his favoured wife and a beloved Pondo princess.

The amaXhosa lived a communal life, with political systems that ensured
everyone shared in its wealth – which was cattle. With cattle, a man would

Instead of being imprisoned behind bars on Robben Island, these Xhosa chiefs served out their sentences in huts covered with tarpaulins.

barter, pay lobola (bridewealth) to seal a marriage or issue rewards. The communal life impacted on governance, too. In a despatch to the colonial authorities in Cape Town, the missionary Rev. H. H. Dugmore wrote: 'The chief's retinue are men who come to him for a time that they may obtain cattle to procure wives, arms or other objects of desire. On obtaining these, they return home and give place to others. Thus the immediate retinue of the chief is continually changing.'

However, the encroachment of British and Boer farmers narrowed the land available to the Khoi and Xhosa. When war failed, witchcraft and superstition began to hold sway.

British traveller George Thompson wrote in 1827 of the amaXhosa that 'prisoners taken in battle and the women and children of the vanquished are uniformly spared. If in their wars with the colonist they have sometimes evinced a more vindictive spirit, it may be questioned whether their ferocity has not been exasperated by the unworthy and cruel treatment they have often experienced from the Christians.'

He recorded an incident in the late 1780s when the 'boors of Bruintjieshoogte invited the Mandankae clan of Caffers, of whom Jalumba was chief, to meet them on the western bank of the Great Fish River to consult on some public matters'. The amiable colonists generously distributed tobacco while they talked. They then said they had gifts for their visitors and laid rush mats on the ground on which they sprinkled mounds of beads. 'The boors retired a little distance to where their guns were lying ready loaded with two or three bullets each. The Caffers rushed upon the beads, overturning each other in their eagerness. The boors seized their guns and poured in a volley upon their unsuspecting visitors; so destructive was their murderous aim that very few escaped the massacre. The residue of the Mandankae immediately abandoned the banks of the Fish River and sought refuge in the Zuurveld with the Chief Congo, and their countrymen of the Tinde tribe.'

Similarly, the adventurer Le Vaillant wrote in 1790, that 'the Caffrees are in general harmless and peaceable, but being continually pillaged, harassed, nay often murdered by the whites, they are obliged to take up arms in their own defence'. He recorded an instance where colonists on a cattle-raiding expedition destroyed all the people of a village but for a 12-year-old child who hid in a hole. A colonist found him and determined to take him for a slave. An argument ensued between the colonist and the leader of the party who said the slave should be his. Finally the leader shouted, 'If I can't have him, then neither can you' and shot the child dead. There were also colonists, Le Vaillant wrote, who would take the survivors of cattle raiding or slaving expeditions and make them stand 'at a stated distance, to try their superiority over each other as expert marksmen'.

PEOPLE UNDER PRESSURE

The Xhosa were being driven into a wedge by British on their east coast, disaffected Boers on their southern borders, the warring Zulu to the north and the inhospitable semidesert of the Karoo to the west. The territory of the Xhosa extended for about 320 kilometres in length by about 90 in breadth, with a population of about 100 000. George Thompson noted: 'Their country is fare more densely populated than any district of the colony ... having been recently dispossessed of the territory between the Keikamma and Fish River, their kraals are now so crowded upon one another, that their is scarcely sufficient pasture for their cattle; and unless they borrow from the colony an improved mode of agriculture, famine must occasionally prevail, till their numbers are reduced to the limits which the country can support.'

In the early 1840s it was estimated that the population density on Chief Ngqika's land was 35 people to every 1,8 square kilometres, while on Chief Sandile's land there were 60 to every 1,8 square killometres. But the white colonists wanted more land. 'They are continually soliciting from the government fresh grants beyond the nominal boundary ... they maintain that the Bushmen are a nation of robbers who, as they neither cultivate the soil, nor pasture cattle, are incapable of occupying their country advantageously (and) would live more comfortably by becoming the herdsmen and household servants of the Christians.'

Thompson received these views from a Boer field commandant, and in reflection penned: 'It struck me as a strange and melancholy trait of human nature, that this Veld-Commandant, in many other points a meritorious, benevolent and clear-sighted man, seemed to be perfectly unconscious that any part of his proceedings, or those of his countrymen, in their wars with the Bushmen, could awaken my abhorrence. The massacre of hundreds of these miserable creatures, and the carrying away of their children into servitude, seemed to be considered by him and his companions as things perfectly lawful, just and necessary, and as meritorious service done to the public, of which they had no more cause to be ashamed, than a brave soldier of having distinguished himself against the enemies of his country; on the other hand, he spoke with detestation of the callousness of the Bushmen in the commission of murder and robbery upon the Christians; not seeming to be aware that the treatment these persecuted tribes had for ages received from Christians, might justify every excess of malice and revenge they were able to perpetrate.'

In the Cape, slavery was abolished in 1833 and 35 000 slaves freed. This was the last straw for many Boers, who harnessed their horses, yoked their oxen to wagons, filled boxes with preserved fruit and dried meat, and set off to govern themselves in the southern African interior.

The event began 80 years of war with African tribes for land, a war probably won by the British in 1913, with the Land Act, when Africans were stripped of their rights to own land. The threat of this law had led to the formation of the African National Congress (ANC) in Bloemfontein a year earlier, an event which began 82 years of struggle.

MAKANA

But almost 100 years before the founding of the ANC there lived a great Xhosa freedom fighter, who became so legendary among the 20th-century political activists of Robben Island that many called it Makana's Island.

Nxele Makana (or Lynks, meaning lefthanded) was mentioned in colonial records as a 'Caffer of intelligence and had some ideas of religion, by professing to be a teacher and prophet, acquired great respect among the adherents of Congo and S'Hlambi's (Ndlambe) party.' Humane and attentive, Makana became the chief counsellor to the most important chiefs. A populist, Makana's greatest influence was a dour Dutch missionary called John Theodore van der Kemp, at whose mission station Makana lived for some years.

Van der Kemp was a succesful businessman and an atheist, until his wife and only child died in a boating accident on the River Maas in Holland. He found solace in religion and, in 1798, three years after the founding of the London Missionary Society, he volunteered to be the first to bring God to the 'Caffres and Hottentots'. Van der Kemp settled in the lands ruled by Chief Ngqika, and his influence spread so fast that Boers hatched a plot to kill him. They sent three assassins on horseback after him on one of his journeys, but pouring rain obliterated his tracks – and enhanced Xhosa legends of his invincibility.

The local people were intensely spiritual. The Xhosa believed in a supreme being, Uhlanga (supreme), while the Khoi called the deity Utika (beautiful). Makana was entranced by the similarities of Christianity to African spiritual beliefs, in particular the resurrection.

Van der Kemp, who married a Khoi woman, died in 1811 in Cape Town. He was 64 and had been a missionary for 13 years. His death coincided with the rise of Makana, his disciple. Makana instructed his followers to abandon harmful herbs, stop adultery and narrate their dreams. A Christian, he sought Xhosa unity and an end to colonialism.

A fascinating account of Makana and his prophecies was given in a narrative from Superintendent G. Cyrus to R. Graham, civil commissioner of Albany in Grahamstown on January 10, 1854, only two years before similar prophecies by Nongquase almost destroyed the amaXhosa. Cyrus noted the recollections of an 80-year-old Fingo man called Gwija who lived in Grahamstown.

Gwija said he had already 'cultivated his field 26 seasons' when word came of a 'doctor whose name they said was Nxele (Makana). We were enjoined to slaughter all our cattle and goats and to destroy our corn.'

Makana promised that if they followed his prophecy their ancestors would be resurrected and the cattle they destroyed would be replaced by strong herds. They did as instructed but nothing happened. 'Our hopes were strengthened by (an unnamed) woman prophet who said Nxele's predictions were about to be realised.' The ancestors had instructed her to summon all the tribes to a cave with offerings for the ancestors. 'The tribes assembled forming a dense three mile long column.' She told them to sing 'Tapo, Siyatandaza Kuwe Umdali Dali' (haste, we pray you, creator of the created). The woman

disappeared into the cave while they sang for hours. She reappeared much later, distraught, saying that as the king of the ancestors was about to put his foot on earth, the boys sent to guide him made a noise which frightened him. Later, she told them to move to another cave, which they did. An old woman came to them and told them to commence a joyful dance, and warned that whoever stopped to rest would fall 'into an everlasting sleep'. The people danced through the night, but still the ancestors did not come. By dawn the chiefs were exhausted and ordered the execution of the false prophets.

Makana remained untouched by these false prophets. His fame soared after Chief Ndlambe, under whom he served as a general and war doctor, came into conflict with Chief Ngqika, who had kidnapped Thuthula, the wife of one of Ndlambe's counsellors. Ngqika refused to return her. Assegaais were sharpened and Makana prepared powerful war muti (medicine). The tribes clashed between the Buffalo

River and the Debe near King William's Town. Losses were heavy. Ngqika called in the colonial authorities, who sent a strong military force to punish Ndlambe and seized huge herds of cattle, giving 9 000 head to Ngqika.

The war spread as the other chiefs retaliated, and small British military encampments had to be evacuated. Makana, with Dusani, assembled Ndlambe, Congo and Habanna to attack Grahamstown. Ngqika warned the British. On April 22, 1819, wave upon wave of young Xhosa warriors fell before British fire

---

These huts were built by Xhosa chiefs imprisoned on Robben Island in the latter half of the 19th century.

as they attacked Grahamstown under Makana. Troops were ordered to take Makana dead or alive. Appalled at the loss in human life, Makana surrendered to the Landdrost at Graaff-Reinet, and was immediately shackled and sent to Robben Island.

Within months, Makana became part of the most famous escape attempt from Robben Island. The plan was masterminded by two prisoners, John Smith and a man called Holmes. Overpowering their guards, a group of prisoners stole a longboat and headed for the closest point to the island, Blaauwberg beach. However, the boat shattered on rocks fringing the beach and most of the men were drowned. Legend has it that Makana clung to a rock shouting encouragement to his comrades before he drowned. But many more chiefs were to become prisoners on the Island.

MAQOMA AND HIS SONS

Chief Maqoma had a large close-knit family, a wife – Kayti – whom he adored and, among his children, two beloved sons, Ned and Kona. The latter gained fame as an African resister of colonialism, and was also imprisoned on Robben Island years after his father.

Ned helped in a hospital run by Dr J. P. Fitzgerald, to whom he gave this account. In 1846, before he or his father were jailed, Kona became seriously ill. Maqoma sent an emissary with a cow as a fee to a witchdoctor named Inata for her to divine who had bewitched his son.

Inata came with her lackeys. Maqoma's counsellors and kinsmen assembled in a circle, while the doctor, with half her face painted white and her upper torso naked, danced in a strange dipping, weaving way around the gathering and sang an incantation called 'Umhobe'. After some time she announced that the poisoner was in the circle and had poisoned some of the red clay used to pain Kona. Panzi, a brave and clever counsellor, saw that suspicion fell on him and fled during the night. The withdoctor said Panzi must be found and killed or he would murder Kona.

Some time later Ned received news that Panzi was back in his kraal. Panzi was seized. A rein was slipped around his neck and a fire lit, and large stones were placed around and within it. While the stones whitened in the heat, Panzi pleaded, 'Give me time and I will give up the poison'. The grip of his accusers slackened; 'Do it', they commanded. He went into his hut and came out with a small piece of rag and said 'This is the poison'. Everyone was too frightened to touch the rag. He confessed, ' I have poisoned others,' and confirmed the names mentioned by the witchdoctor. Panzi was grabbed and placed, belly first, on the hot stones. His screams rent the air, which filled with the pungent smell of burning flesh. He cried: 'Let me get the other poison.' His accusers pulled him off the stones, and as they did, skin fell off in strips from his belly and thighs. Panzi staggered to his hut and, picking up a stone, said, 'This is the poison I killed others with.' He said that after people moved from a sitting place on the ground he placed the stone where they had sat, and this bewitched them. He said he had got the stone from Peo, a counsellor from another tribe who was killed for bewitching his chief. Panzi was thrust on his back across the fire to force him to give up all the poison. He screamed that he would show them more poison, struggled to his feet with huge blisters scouring flesh off his back and legs and crawled to his hut where he dug up rubbish and said it was all he had. He was hanged from a tree and his corpse thrown into the river.

When the commandant of the Native Police, Mr Davis, heard of the incident he jailed some of the men involved. Ned fled with 20 armed men into the bush determined to fight rather than be arrested. He lived in this way for three months.

At last, he went to Kona and said he wanted to give himself up. Kona would not consent. But after a few more weeks he became tired – as only fugitives can be, and when arrest seems a refuge from fear. Ned went to missionary Charles Brownlee and gave himself up. He was fined 10 head of cattle.

SANDILE AND SIYOLO

But more serious calamities were awaiting the chiefs, and this time the focus was on Sandile. Governor Sir Harry Smith received a letter from Major Somerset at Fort Hare on January 27, 1851, warning of a 'large combined force of Sandili's kaffirs and others, the rebel hottentots of the Blinkwater, and all the Gonah forces who were under the later "Hermanus" are more or less under Sandile's orders and Maqoma'. He said the warriors extended west from the Chumie mountains to the Winterberg mountains and by the Kaga Berg to the Fish River, cutting off all direct communications, and 'leaving all the farms in that line of country in the complete possession of the enemy'.

The townsfolk of Albany wrote to Governor Smith on June 7, 1851, calling for more troops to protect them. They claimed Sandile 'has directed his warriors to enter the colony during the winter months to lay waste, destroy and plunder in every direction'. Smith wrote from King William's Town five days later that he would establish a commission to investigate 'the inexplicable disaffection of the coloured people and their fraternisation with the kafirs – their hereditary enemies who drove them from their country'. He pointed out that the coloureds 'enjoyed every privilege accorded to the most favoured people, they live under the laws of the colony and possess the civil and religious rights of British subjects. They are provided with pastors and teachers.'

Why, then, were they so ungrateful? The commission reported that 'their (the Khoi and coloured people) strange revolt is to be traced to some feeling of ancient right to the whole of the land on the confines of which they now hold but a nook'.

In November 1851, the men of Siyolo, chief of the Ndlambe Xhosa, cut down 60 men of the inexperienced Queen's Regiment in the Fish River Bush, the greatest loss of life by a British regiment in any engagement of the War of Mlanjeni (1850-53), also known as the Eighth Frontier War.

Sir Harry Smith was replaced by Governor George Cathcart, and he received instructions a month later, on February 2, 1852, that war against the 'Hottentots and Kafres should be prosecuted with unremitting vigour until it can be finished by their being reduced to complete and unconditional submission'. By October, 1852, Siyolo had been captured, like Hintsa and Sandile before him, by promises of negotiations and a just end to conflict; instead he was sent to Robben Island for 17 years.

THE PROPHETS

The Cape Colony was enjoying relative prosperity when Sir George Grey arrived in 1854, so he turned his attention to the destruction of the chiefs of Natal and British Kaffraria.

'Awazwi kam-Hala kuyo inkosi enkulu ka-Rumente' – the words of Chief Umhala to the 'great chief of the government' (Chief Commissioner Colonel Maclean) – began a letter dated 13 March, 1856, from Umhala. The British translation of his words, affixed to his letter, encapsulate the frustrations of the Xhosa chiefs at the despicable treatment they received from petty magistrates: 'The police who run the guns, whose permission did he ask? (They should have asked a chief for permission to enter his territory.) His people, the unbelievers, who did not kill, are coming to (Major) Gawler, they did not acquaint him (Umhala) of it. Umhala says he never enters Gawler's house. Gawler drives him away, although petty chiefs and common people are permitted to enter. Another white man must come who is good. Gawler treats Umhala wrongly, he will bring war upon this country.' His frustrated appeal fell on deaf ears. Instead, Sir George Shepstone decreed that Fingo labourers should be employed in East London at a higher rate of wages than Africans, 'because the kafirs have indolent natures'. The Xhosa turned to prophecy again.

The wife of Bula, one of Chief Kama's counsellors, said in April 1856 that the Russians then fighting the British in the Crimean War would come to help them. Instead, Maqoma was jailed on Robben Island not long after drafting a heartfelt plea to Sir George Grey, with Chief Botman: 'We have often written to you but received no reply ... Where is the land we can live together on? It is not with our consent, for if we refused, you would think we make a fight with you, sir. I'm cry to you much from a desire to meet you that we may state our complaints.'

A year later, Nongqase, the bright 15-year-old niece of Chief Kwitchi, a counsellor of Umhala, said that if the Xhosa stopped planting, burned their crops, killed their cattle and destroyed their ornaments, the British would be driven into the sea. Kona ignored these prophecies, but could not escape the desperate desire of other Xhosa to rid the land of white settlers. In March, 1857, he had to move his people from near Fort Murray to Tzatzoe's location to protect their cattle from those who were slaying cattle in accord with Nongqase's prophecy.

Mass starvation resulted from the great cattle killing, forcing many to go to the towns to work. To regulate this sudden spate of workers, the pass (or influx control) laws of 1853 were extended in 1856. Every magistrate had to keep a register of 'all native applicants for service'. It was the earliest form of labour bureau, which would be used by the 20th-century apartheid government and the great mining houses to recruit and control African workers.

By late 1857 dry stalks withered where grain fields had been, and the bleached bones of slain cattle lay across barren fields. Some 28 892 Xhosa were forced off the land to register at the labour bureaus. The Xhosa hated city work, and as the next year's crops grew ready for harvest and the herds built up, applications for work dropped to 7 519, and fell to 358 the year after.

CAPTURE AND HUMILIATION

And now came the final humiliation of the chiefs and the methodical destruction of the amaXhosa. Many of the most influential chiefs and their counsellors were arrested from September 1857 onward, and held in King William's Town jail. Minor charges were laid against them. The paranoid Grey saw Nongqase's prophecies as a 'great conspiracy against the European race'. The racist Major Gawler (that Umhala complained of) suggested a 'clean sweep of all the chiefs, but we must work cautiously and with certainty'.

The same month, Chief Xhoxho and two counsellors were sentenced to three years in jail for allowing an ox to be slaughtered at Xhoxho's kraal and eating its meat. Chief Pato and his son Mpaga were sentenced to five years on Robben Island while Delima was sentenced to seven years. The following month, Nongqase and her uncle Chief Kwitchi were sent to Robben Island for a decade. On November 12, Chief Xaimpi was sentenced to Robben Island. On his way to trial, he asked his arresting officers to stop within sight of King William's Town, and, using a trick passed down in lore from Makana, he took a piece of wood from his pouch, chewed it, spat it out, and then jumped facing a number of directions. Unfortunately for Xaimpi, Makana's magic failed, and he remained sufficiently visible to his jailers to be sentenced to 14 years for being an accessory to the theft of two horses. While on the island, another seven years was added to his sentence for attempting to escape. Chief Sandile, living out a miserable existence among the lepers, chronically ill and the insane of Robben Island, soon had plenty of contemporaries from the African chieftanships of the amaXhosa and amaZulu sharing his misery.

In November 1857, colonial forces succeeded in capturing Maqoma and others. He was sentenced to death for his part in the murder of a headman, even though the magistrate and others close to the case confided in personal letters that it was clear he had no part in the crime. But it was politically expedient to get him out of the way. Grey commuted the sentence to 20 years on Robben Island.

Umhala was tracked down and jailed in June 1858 for receiving stolen cattle and furthering the prophecies of Nongqase. He was sent, like the chiefs before him – manacled hand and foot – from Port Elizabeth via Breakwater prison in Cape Town to Robben Island. Like the ANC and PAC prisoners a century later, the Xhosa chiefs found their chains so tight and heavy that their wrists and ankles bled. A year later, in May, Chief Stock was sentenced to seven years on the Island.

ISLAND OF CHIEFS

Within two years, the Xhosa nation had been crushed by superstition and duplicity. All the major Xhosa chiefs were now living in huts made of tarpaulin and saplings near Murray's Bay on Robben Island. They hunted birds, rabbits and dassies and were allowed some goats. Siyolo and Maqoma were acccompanied by their wives, but many wives, including those of Umhala and Xhoxho, refused to join their husbands. This loss of family was as grievous as the loss of their land. The prisoners made vain appeals to be released. The wives of Siyolo and Maqoma smuggled messages back to Xhosaland in a vain bid to maintain links with their homeland. Maqoma's beloved wife, Katyi, fell ill and refused medication, telling the doctor, 'No, my heart is sore. I want to die.' The chiefs were joined by Tyali, Maqoma's brother, who was jailed for theft and contracted leprosy on the Island. Chief Xidon had an ulcer. Chief Sinanda went blind. Chief Nkhola lost an arm.

In 1869, the last of the chiefs, Maqoma, Siyolo and Xhoxho, were released. They returned to a land that had lost its soul. Their people were scattered and their lands belonged to German, Dutch and English settlers. They were not allowed to own land or to summon their followers. A heartbroken and stubborn Maqoma, now a very old man, twice tried to return to his lands. The irritated colonial authorities, tiring of him, sent him back to Robben Island.

Maqoma's spirit was perhaps already dead, and after 18 months he surrendered to a higher authority. He died, an old great warrior, his face creased with the history of his nation and eyes red with the tears of a hundred years. The Anglican chaplain who was with him said he died 'of old age and dejection, at being here alone, no wife, or child, or attendant'.

Within two years the Xhosa chiefs were replaced on the Island by Zulu chiefs. A letter from the Lord Bishop of Natal to the Cape authorities in January 1875 requested privileges for 'ex-chief Lungelibalile' and his son. These were granted: they were allowed fish as well as meat, and coffee or tea daily. Additional expenses were charged to the government of Natal.

By 1877 the last Frontier War – or as Govan Mbeki (a historian and former 20th-century Robben Islander) called them, the Wars of Dispossession – had begun. The sons of Sandile, Umhala and Maqoma – including the brave Kona – were among the first of the next generation of Xhosa leaders to take their places on Robben Island. By 1879, black political prisoners were again swelling the Island prison's population (as they would exactly 100 years later). There were four Galeka prisoners of war at Murray's Bay and 11 Koranna prisoners in a room adjoining the convict station. The Island sewers could not cope and kept bursting, leading to outbreaks of typhoid.

The story of Maqoma does not end with his death. On July 23, 1978, the *Sunday Tribune* reported that Chief Jongumsobombu Maqoma's bones were being moved from Cape Town by the *SA Navy*, to be buried in Heroes' Acre in the Tyume Valley, Ciskei. The Xhosa historian, Chief S. M. Burns-Ncamashe of Rhodes University, argued that it was tradition to bury a chief on the spot where he lost his life in battle. He said to remove Maqoma's bones would be to rob him of the honour he deserved. Nonetheless, Xhosa seer Charity Sonandi divined where he was buried on the Island, and when his remains arrived at Port Elizabeth harbour aboard a naval gunboat on August 6, 1978, a crowd of more than 2 000 waited to welcome the lonely warrior home.

.THE SECOND
WORLD WAR

*'There is no need for wars or violence, under any circumstances.
There are no problems that cannot be solved around a table,
provided there is good will and reciprocal trust
or even reciprocal fear.'*
Primo Levi, Auschwitz survivor, 'The Drowned and The Saved', 1986

For aeons, Robben Island has guarded the approaches to Table Bay. In the past four centuries, the Island has often served as a defence outpost, in addition to its roles as buffer, refuge and beacon. In the days of sail, messages left under appointed rocks by mariners provided intelligence for fellow merchant seamen. When the machinations of European power politics brought France and Britain together against Holland in 1672, orders went out that posts at Saldanha Bay and at Robben Island should be abandoned at the first appearance of the enemy. Women, children and cattle at those outposts were sent to the Castle in Cape Town. But the isolated Dutch possession at the southern tip of Africa was of little interest to generals carving new boundaries in Europe at the time.

However, during the Second World War, the Germans and Japanese were not blind to the opportunities offered by the Cape. The importance of the shipping route round the Cape of Good Hope saw Robben Island don military attire during the Second World War as its role as a strategic guardsman again became important.

PREPARING FOR WAR

Two huge guns, each capable of firing a 385-pound projectile for a distance of 32 kilometres, became the mainstay of the Island's defences. They were originally positioned on Signal Hill. However, when the guns were fired the concussion was so intense that windows shattered for miles around, and the 1928 Committee on Imperial Defence ordered them moved to Robben Island.

A decade later, with war in Europe on the horizon, South Africa's Defence Minister, Oswald Pirow, told Parliament that Cape Town would be made 'battleship proof' with a battery of 15-inch guns on Robben Island. Because the Suez Canal was considered vulnerable to attack, the Cape had already been recognised as potentially significant to the war effort. Britain was helping to pay for the new Duncan Dock in Cape Town, but Pirow suggested improved facilities could increase the risk of attack.

British Prime Minister Winston Churchill did not agree. Churchill wrote to Prime Minister Jan Smuts that the defences of Cape Town and Simonstown fell far short of the recommendations of the 1928 Committee on Imperial Defence. He noted that although South Africa considered the Robben Island 15-inch battery extravagant, Britain would arrange early delivery of a further two-gun battery of high-angle 9.2-inch guns for the Island. One of these was installed by naval artillery personnel in 1940. It had a battle weight of around 10 tons and took seven people to fire it. Three other guns, two Mark 7s and one Mark 9, were erected in 1944. The guns, concealed in the bluegum plantations, were fired during a practice run and ignited the trees across the north of the Island in a totally unintentional but nonetheless impressive blaze.

By 1940, war preparations on Robben Island were intense, but the logistics of battle preparedness for the Island were a nightmare. *Issie*, a little steamer named in honour of Jan Smuts's wife, could ferry no more than 45 people at a time to and from the Island. There were no seats, and passengers had to hold on for dear life while *Issie*, belching black smoke and tumbling through the swells, would take an hour to reach its destination. Work began on a jetty at Murray's Bay to facilitate the landing of stores and heavy

Abandoned World War II barracks provided rough shelter for the soldiers stationed on Robben Island.

equipment for further fortifications. The Coast Artillery Brigade Headquarters at Cape Town was replaced on 8 February, 1940 by the Cape Peninsula Artillery Brigade Headquarters at the Castle, with First Heavy Battery on the mainland and Fifth Heavy Battery on Robben Island.

At the time, South Africa's ground defence against hostile aircraft consisted of a battery of obsolete 3-inch guns and the machine guns of the South African Air Force, whose own operational strength was limited to several dozen old biplane fighters and 18 modern Junkers, which were later converted to bombers.

EARLY DAYS

The Women's Auxiliary Army Service (WAAS) became the core of the Island's early wartime administration staff, initially under Sergeant Bridgette McCall. She spent 18 months on the Island, from mid-1941 to late 1942, and within days of leaving the Island for duty in Cape Town, met a young man recently returned from North Africa. The two had a whirlwind courtship and in March, 1943, Bridgette McCall became the bride of one of the wealthiest and most eligible bachelors in the world, Harry Oppenheimer.

Bridgette had enjoyed her time on the Island. Unlike most of the women, who were housed in barracks, she had a room to herself. It was sparse, with bare floors and a naked light bulb, but it was home. The only irritant was the nearby foghorn, which kept her awake during the frequent thick mists around the Island, as it bleated its warning to ships.

Her private quarters were more comfortable than the tented camps which were home to the soldiers undergoing training on the Island, many of whom were coloured servicemen of the Cape Corps. These servicemen lived in a camp separate from white soldiers. Despite its name, the Cape Corps attracted recruits from as far away as the Witwatersrand. A total of 45 015 coloured men (including Indian and Malay units) served in the Cape Corps – both in South Africa and overseas – during the Second World War. Some 4 584 men of the Cape Corps fought against Italian fascist forces in Ethiopia where they served with distinction.

However, on the Island, although they would often drill long after they were required to, Bridgette Oppenheimer recalls that not all were happy. One day she received a call in her office about a young coloured recruit who had shot himself on a beach on the other side of the Island. No ambulance crew was available so she and a young officer, neither of whom had medical training, leapt into the ambulance and drove to the shale-strewn northern beach where the recruit lay with a bullet wound in the head. The two carefully picked him up and placed him in the ambulance. The man was still conscious. Bridgette drove while the other officer sat with the man. 'He said, "drive carefully, I'm in great pain."' By the time they reached the village he was dead. 'It was very sad. I was only 19 and had never seen anyone die before,' she recalls.

Not long after this tragedy, the first draft of 400 Cape Corps gunners from Robben Island – who had never handled a rifle, and only saw a Bofors gun (a Swedish-made anti-aircraft gun) days before going into combat in Abyssinia – were ferried to the mainland and went by train to Durban, where they boarded ships for the Middle East. Table talk around Cape Town was derisory about these recruits, with people taking bets on how many would abscond during the journey from the Cape to Durban. However, when the first roll call was taken after embarkation in Durban it was found that the commanding officer did not have 400 Cape Corps soldiers, he had 401.

Within a few weeks of reporting to 1st Light Anti-Aircraft Regiment in Ethiopia, a number of Cape Corps soldiers had been killed or taken prisoner. In November 1941, the Cape Corps fought alongside the rest of the 5th South African Infantry Brigade during the fierce struggle at Sidi Rezegh in Libya where, with captured Italian rifles, they faced the tanks of the German Afrika Korps. The arrival of new military weaponary from 2nd Light Anti-Aircraft Regiment saw most survivors join this regiment and take part in the battle for Bardia in 1942.

Not all could be absorbed by the 1st Light Anti-Aircraft Regiment, and after many were dumped in the Non-European Army Services Camp, discontent arose among the men of the Cape Corps. They had responded willingly to appeals for recruits. During the First World War, the unit had been an infantry regiment – a fighting unit – that had distinguished itself in the campaigns in East Africa and Palestine. The policy of the government and military administration had changed by 1940, however, and most coloured and 'native' volunteers were assigned to white units for 'service' duties, such as stretcher-bearers, drivers, labourers and cooks. Those who had hoped to regain the martial distinctions won by their fathers were bitterly disappointed. But, despite official policy, many found themselves in the firing line; others manned coastal artillery batteries, while a relatively small number served afloat with the fledgling South African Navy.

COASTAL DEFENCE

While its soldiers were fighting bravely across the seas, South Africa's coastal defences were in disarray. The entry of Japan into the war in late 1941 saw South African paranoia heighten. The Japanese quickly occupied Hong Kong,

World War II soldiers would have positioned themselves in outposts such as these to defend the Island from hostile invaders if German U-boats patrolling Cape waters had landed.

landed in the Philippines, pushed into Burma through Thailand and – to the joy of the neo-Nazi Ossewabrandwag (OB) in South Africa – captured Singapore, which meant the loss of Allied docking facilities there. The fall of Singapore increased the importance of Durban and Cape Town. Plans for the Sturrock Graving Dock at Cape Town were brought forward. German U-boats were already having regular rendezvous on the Natal coast with neo-Nazis, such as the OB, to foment internal anti-British, pro-Nazi intelligence-gathering and sabotage. Military tacticians believed the Japanese might attempt to conquer Mozambique or Madagascar to sever Allied lines of communication with the Middle East and Far East.

By 1941, the Germans began to lay deadly magnetic mines in their offensive against Allied shipping. In response to this threat, naval authorities established a 'degaussing' range on the east of the Island, in the Blaauwberg Channel. The process of degaussing involved neutralising the magnetic field of a ship's hull by circling it with a current-carrying electric cable. By war's end, degaussing teams on the Island had protected thousands of ships. The Island was also the control centre for the submarine detection cables that stretched to Melkbosstrand and Clifton.

Cape Town had its first air raid alarm on the night of November 24, 1941, when a gun positioned on Robben Island reported three unidentified aircraft at 11:15 p.m. At 12:55 a.m. troops on Green Point Common saw a yellow light moving from west to east. Various other reports, from a sound locator at Camps Bay, from the docks and from Lion Battery, put the entire military corps on red alert. At 2:30 a.m., the 'all clear' signal was given.

Bridgette Oppenheimer recalls the incident well; she was working at SACS school in the cipher officer under General I. P. de Villiers and was privy to some of the most sensitive information in the Cape. She recalls that when the aircraft was detected, all hell broke loose with fears of a Japanese attack. However, they soon realised that the enemy aircraft was no more than a young aviator who had over-imbibed and taken his aircraft up for an unauthorised flip across the night skies. He did not receive a friendly welcome when he landed. But he had caused enough panic to ensure that on three other occasions that month fighter aircraft were scrambled to intercept other aircraft. Nought arose from any of these over-reactions from a hitherto comfortably sleepy command.

The sense of distance and security South Africans felt, far from the war, was proved by a large-scale mobilisation of volunteer forces on October 4, 1942: there was only 54% attendance in East London and 50% in Cape Town and Port Elizabeth. Ten hours after the mobilisation was called in Durban, only a third of the potential force had pitched up. One Coast Defence Corps battalion, which had to move from Table Bay to Robben Island on a stomach-churning voyage on board *Issie*, had landed only a quarter of its strength more than eight hours after the emergency callup. There was such despair among officers at this pathetic turnout that they decided to cut the strength of the Coast Defence Corps battalions to six. Disaster struck only a day later.

THE UNDERSEA THREAT

By 1942, with the Mediterranean a battleground, convoys carrying reinforcements and war material were rounding the Cape in a constant stream. The German High Command in Berlin sought to curb this flow; around August 20, 1942, German naval authorities sent four U-boats from Lorient in France to attack shipping in South African waters. A submarine tanker, U-459, accompanied these undersea hunters.

On their way to the Cape along the west coast of Africa, the submarines sank the troopship *Laconia*, carrying 1 800 Italian prisoners of war en route from South Africa to Britain. One submarine was damaged by a US bomber, but the remaining three refuelled at night to the south of Walvis Bay and headed for the Cape.

Not long after, the Submarine Tracking Room at the Admiralty in London warned of seven U-boats near Cape Town. On October 5 – the day after South African troops had mostly ignored the mock mobilisation – the submarine U-68 was 40 kilometres off Cape Town, within view of Table Mountain. That night, Captain Carl Emmerman, commander of U-172, surfaced and headed toward Table Bay. He stopped within hailing distance of Robben Island and allowed the crew up, one by one, to enjoy the diamante sparkle of a city unconcerned with wartime blackouts, before submerging again.

Early the next afternoon Emmerman brought his U-boat in closer, and lay at periscope depth in calm water between Robben Island and Green Point. Brilliant sunshine flecked prisms of light off the sea. The harbour installations studied by Emmerman were perfectly etched against the skyline. There was no response from the mainland to this threat.

Berlin's order to start operations followed quickly. The next day, October 7, Emmerman sank the *Firethorn* and, the day after, torpedoed the *Chickasaw City*, 96 kilometres from Cape Town. His fellow U-boat commanders blew up another eight Allied ships in the next two days. A SAAF Ventura bomber was finally cranked into the air and destroyed one of the submarines, but Cape defences spent more time picking up survivors than fighting the enemy.

Once he had struck fear into the hearts of seafarers using the Cape shipping route, Emmerman and his flotilla cruised back to Europe. Like a string of rubies, their route could be threaded together in a series of explosions as they torpedoed ships along the African coast.

LIFE DURING WARTIME

For the members of the Women's Auxiliary Army Service (WAAS) and the Women's Auxiliary Naval Service (SWANS) – who arrived in 1943 – Island life, but for the small disturbances of the occasional U-boat commander, was fun. Apart from their official duties, there were with long walks in the bracing wind and frequent dances. They would dine at scrubbed wooden tables, seated on hard benches, or relax in wicker chairs in a sparsely furnished common room. On Fridays they would push the chairs to one side, wind up the gramophone and dance. The men of the Cape Corps were not invited to these events, and the women so outnumbered the men that one woman wrote what a privilege it was to be asked to dance by a man.

Toilets were outside the bungalows and few doors had locks. Women performed their ablutions while clinging to the door. During one howling southeaster, a toilet door was whipped from the hands of a young radar operator, who watched in fascination as the wind tossed it across the Island.

One set of stone bungalows with painted-over windows were called 'worse to putrid'. The iron beds were so close together that if you rolled over at night you could find yourself in a neighbour's bed. The roofs leaked, naked light bulbs swayed and furnishings were basic. The women tried to grow flowers, but their gardens withered in the dry, glistening sand. To try and cheer things up, some women would pipe dance music softly over the camp speakers early in the mornings after the wake-up was trumpeted.

The SWANS were excellent harbour defence operators. The first radar installation on the Island, Windy Ridge, was set up in a leaky tent in 1943, and was finally housed in a gloomy high-walled building near the old Leper Cemetery. Month-long technical training courses were held for 30 women at a time. Cynthia Smuts recalled going for training on a coastal artillery course held on Robben Island in July, 1943. In Peter Brain's book, *SA Radar in World War 2*, she recalls that *Issie* 'bounced and rolled merrily through the winter sea'. Less merry was a cargo of rancid Australian butter that did nothing to help the sea sickness passengers experienced.

'We received a frosty welcome from a very smart Artillery "madam" who looked with displeasure at her dishevelled trainees. Our barracks were in the basement of a dingy old building which once housed lepers.'

The women were subject to drills and frequent route marches. One beautiful spring day in August they went marching up a low hill 'with yellow mimosas weighing down wet trees and arum lilies and chincherinchees breaking through the damp grass'. As they came to the top of the hill they saw a convoy at anchor. 'The ships were weighed down on the landward side by hundreds of men in battledress hanging over the rails, smoking, chatting and enjoying the sun. They were close to the Island and the sudden appearance of 20 marching girls delighted them. They broke into yells and whoops, waving and whistling.'

After the war, the Navy retained control of the Island until 1958. Life returned to normal, although the Island was still an active base for a small force of naval gunners and their families. The Island mascot was a mongrel called Tackline, which one officer recalls 'was a stupid dog'. *Issie* survived the evolution of the the Island from army fortress to naval base to a maximum security prison for 'African male political prisoners'. She retired in 1976 after 34 years of service and was bought as an amusement for children at a Cape Town nursery school where she still endures their games.

THE LAST DAY
OF OCTOBER

*'I have to remember everything, keep track of
blades of grass, the threads of the untidy
event, and the houses, inch by inch,
the long lines of the railway,
the textured face of pain.'*

PABLO NERUDA, 'MEMORY', 1973

Ireen Mhlongo bought a double grave site for her and Wilton Mkwayi. But, he says, he is very sorry, he will not be buried next to Ireen amid the thick grasses and red mud of Avalon Cemetery in Soweto. No, when he dies he wants to be cremated. His family can put a teaspoon of his ashes on Ireen's grave, but the rest must be scattered in the seas around Robben Island. Mkwayi spent more years there as a political prisoner than any other place, and it is there that he wants his spirit to rest. His eyes twinkle as he leans on the black railings around Ireen's grave. Besides, he says, the fish will come and swallow his ashes and maybe once racists eat those fish with his ashes in their belly they will forego discrimination. His laugh resonates through the musky khakibos and across the cypresses and palms of Soweto's graveyard.

The love story of Ireen Mhlongo and Wilton Mkwayi is one of the great romances of South Africa. Theirs was a love that refused to allow time nor separation, cruelty nor danger, to dilute it. As constant as the slow spin of the earth, Ireen's love was the axis on which Wilton Mkwayi leant to weather political persecution and increase the commitment to which he gave his life, and ultimately hers. They first met at a party in Soweto in 1956. A brash young political star, he told her he would steal her heart from another. Ireen, being a woman with a mind of her own, promptly went off and married that other man.

But the story of Wilton and Ireen perhaps began when Wilton's father, a peasant, signed 17-year-old Wilton and his three brothers up as members of the African National Congress (ANC). Wilton had left school, like so many of his generation, after Standard Four and worked first as a labourer, then as an 'office boy', then as a factory worker and trade unionist. By 1947, the name Wilton Mkwayi was well known in the Port Elizabeth townships. He was an energetic leader and organiser in the Port Elizabeth bus boycotts, the Defiance Campaign and the Congress of the People. Even in his late '70s he would travel the rutted paths and tracks of Transkei and the midlands of the Eastern

Cape organising rural people and listening to their complaints. Wilton Mkwayi spent his 70th birthday – December 17, 1993 – in Ciskei with his brother's family, and spent the days thereafter travelling to the rural people preparing them for the April 1994 elections and noting their complaints, whether about the dangers of bush pigs or a lack of fresh water. His determination to organise for the ANC and see civil rights extended to all made it not surprising that he was among the 156 charged by the government with treason in 1956. Each day, he travelled from Soweto to Pretoria with 155 co-accused in a trial that would drag on and on before all were acquitted in 1960.

A Port Elizabeth nursing friend, scolding him for his romantic exploits in the eastern Cape, told him she hoped that in Johannesburg he would meet a nurse called Ireen Mhlongo. 'There is a girl who won't agree with you, she will fix you.' It was a challenge that intrigued the popular young politician. At the party where they finally met, Ireen had come direct from work at Baragwanath Hospital in her starched white uniform. She laughed when the handsome 33-year-old told her he would take her away from her boyfriend.

Wilton became immersed in his trial and in underground politics. In 1960, he secretly travelled to Europe and Africa on trade union missions for the South African Congress of Trade Unions (SACTU), and trained in China in the use of small arms. On his return, he worked to establish Umkhonto we Sizwe (MK) with friends and comrades Nelson Mandela, Walter Sisulu and others.

Wilton recalls: 'In 1963, I was in Orlando Extension and asked someone who knew Ireen what she was doing. They said she had divorced.' Seven years after he had first met her, he immediately went to visit her at Meadowlands Clinic, where she then worked, and began a great love affair.

But with love came betrayal. A young man, Bartholomew Tlhapane, who worked closely with Wilton in the ANC, was a keen recruit with a particular interest in MK. Tlhapane was trusted: He acted as co-ordinator of South African Communist Party (SACP) cells and was a fulltime organiser for the SACP and ANC. Wilton made a crucial error by confiding to Tlhapane that if ever he needed to be found urgently, he could be located at Ireen's house. Tlhapane was the only person he gave this information to, and it would lead to the downfall of both.

RIVONIA

The heat was on for the MK High Command, of which Mkwayi was a part, and little mistakes began forming a patchwork of error that would lead to nearly three decades in jail. But Wilton was lulled for a long time by the impression that luck was with him. On July 11, 1963, the day of the Lilliesleaf raid, Wilton was in Soweto making arrangements to smuggle MK recruits out of the country. At that time, the growth of the ANC's underground army had reached a critical phase.

Govan Mbeki described it in a discussion document on MK that was sent around cells on Robben Island years later: 'By the end of 1962 most units could not operate as they did not have the materials with which to carry out their sabotage activities. It was clear that MK had to enter a new phase. The National High Command (NHC) decided to couple sabotage activities with military action. Operation Mayibuye was devised and accepted by the NHC, who submitted it for comment to the joint executives of the ANC and SACP. The comrades who had returned from China (including Mkwayi) were each assigned to take charge of certain operational areas.'

MK needed a headquarters to produce logistical material. 'These headquarters were at Travalyn where all the National High Command were stationed after they left Rivonia. The property was bought under a pseudonym by Dennis Goldberg (and) was 10 minutes from Rivionia along the road to Hartebeespoort.' A week before July 11, the MK High Command moved their belongings from Lilliesleaf farm to Travalyn. The July 11 meeting at Lilliesleaf was important, and because Travalyn was top secret, they decided to gather in the tranquil confines of a small picture-perfect English cottage among the dry Highveld grasses of Lilliesleaf farm.

The meeting was scheduled for 4:00 p.m. Minutes before, Wilton was dropped a few blocks away by a friend. Rivonia was still a rural settlement distant from Johannesburg, with farm land and sprawling bungalows. Wilton did not approach the farm directly, but walked along a footpath that wound along the boundary of Lilliesleaf and another farm. The sun flecked the tips of the waist-high veld grass into shimmering shards of copper and gold, a cowbell tinkled from a grazing herd and the sound of a nearby river gently massaged the ear. It was a warm winter afternoon. No bird stirred in the trees.

'I saw two dogs near the bushes. They looked like our dogs. I thought my chaps wanted to frighten me. I didn't even think of the police.' A little further on he saw what he thought were the same two dogs. It briefly occurred to him that he hadn't noticed the grass rustle as they moved through it.

Two majestic old oak trees with thick trunks guarded the main gates and spilled acorns over the entrance. As Wilton approached, instinct made him remain on the path instead of going a shorter, more direct route. He saw another two dogs. His pace slowed and his heart began to pound; something was not right. He saw another two dogs. His hands felt clammy. He became aware of every blade of grass, every sound, every smell. The soft tones of the dying sun took on sharp contours as his brain recorded everything. He jumped over the fence to the next farm where cattle were gazing and began herding them. It was then that he saw policemen.

Quelling an urge to run, he herded the cattle toward a river that led to Alexandra, keeping close to the water to destroy his scent if dogs followed. In Alexandra he borrowed a car and driver from a fellow ANC activist, had the driver take him to Orlando East and then told the driver to fill up the car and go back to Alexandra. He was laying a dud trail.

Wilton hastened through the deep purple dusk of Soweto, hazed by thousands of coal fires, to a friend's home in Mzimhlope. He twiddled the dials of a radio, listening to news broadcasts. That night there was no news of any arrests or of the raid. The next morning, though, Radio Zulu was the first to carry news of the Rivonia arrests and that Wilton Mkwayi was being sought after being spotted on a neighbouring farm.

At noon he told his friends he was going to fetch some parcels at Park Station and left. Three hours later police knocked on the door

'Do you know Mkwayi?' they asked the daughter of his friend.

'Yes, but I last saw him in 1960,' the savvy teenager answered.

'Have you not seen him since then?' the police demanded.

'I read in the newspaper once that he addressed a meeting in Moroka,' she ventured in the vague, recollective way of adolescence.

The police walked to their van and asked someone inside: 'Didn't you say that when Mkwayi is in Soweto he stays here?' The hidden person assented but nonetheless the disgruntled police left.

Wilton had moved a short distance away to the home of an ANC supporter in Orlando Extension. From here he worked hard recruiting and ushering new cadres out of the country to join MK.

'I didn't want to go to any old contacts, it had become too dangerous. I had to create new cells which was very difficult.' Wilton was puzzled by the lack of news about their lodgings at Travalyn and realised his compatriots – Walter Sisulu, Nelson Mandela, Elias Motsoaledi, Raymond Mhlaba and others – had not revealed it yet.

He consulted with Pieter Byleveld and Braam Fischer, committed ANC supporters who would later pay for their commitment with prison. Mkwayi decided he would risk salvaging as many documents and other material as he could from Travalyn. He went back to Travalyn along the only route he knew, past Lilliesleaf which was still crawling with policemen.

He had lost the keys and had to break a window to open the door. Nothing had been disturbed. With the car engine running outside, he searched Travalyn and found documents and letters about MK activities and routes, but nothing about Operation Mayibuye, the prize that both he and the police sought. He left, but anxiety got the better of him and he returned some days later and searched more carefully. Stray dogs had already taken up residence and the contents of a garbage bin lay strewn about. As he searched, fine dust rose and sparkled in the sun before slowly subsiding. Fearful about staying too long at Travalyn, Wilton pulled blankets off beds, and emptied the contents of drawers into them, so he could take them home to search more carefully. His frantic search for Operation Mayibuye, the ANC's blueprint for armed insurrection, was fruitless. Some of the clothes he recovered were sent as a change of garment to his comrades, who were being held in terms of 90-day detention clauses. Mbeki recalls that when they recognised clothing from Travalyn, 'there was jubilation'.

Mkwayi went back a third, and last, time. 'Braam and Pieter were now saying to me, "you are looking for trouble". Each time I went I found more things, but not what I really wanted'. Days later, in early September, newspapers reported that Travalyn had been uncovered. The previous owner had come to the cottage at the end of August to find out why Dennis Goldberg was defaulting on payments. He found stray dogs, broken windows and no car in the garage. Fearing a crime, he rushed to the police.

Goldberg, he told them, had probably been robbed and murdered and his body disposed of. The police knew better: Goldberg was being questioned with Mandela and others of the MK High Command at Pretoria security branch headquarters. The police were luckier than Mkwayi. They ripped open mattresses and found ANC literature, including a letter from ANC headquarters to MK discussing military matters, and a plan for infiltrating cadres through Botswana.

The delighted police called it 'small Rivonia'. Braam Fischer, who was the lawyer for the trailists, was pleased, too. Mkwayi recalls: 'He sighed and said: "I am glad you did not find that letter. It will prove the ANC is not taking instruction from the Communist Party. There will be no hangings because of that letter."'

Wilton realised his days outside prison and within the country might be numbered, so worked even harder building ANC cells and sending cadres outside the country for military training or to study. Wearing a priest's black cassock and white collar, he travelled to Cape Town, Port Elizabeth, East London, Bloemfontein and Durban. He would form two new MK units in an area, instruct them to form more and move on. Government and white public hysteria about MK had made the organisation even more attractive to young militants and interest in membership soared. But as a security precaution Wilton tightened up selection criteria: only the most trustworthy could join or be sent into exile. A pattern established itself then that would remain for all of MK's underground existence: 'more people wanted to go for military training than to study'.

On September 30, 1964, Wilton was hastening through the rutted roads of Meadowlands to a 'safe house' where he would meet new MK recruits. Unseen by him a group of tsotsis (township thugs) were arguing. A shot exploded in the night sky and funnelled through the muscles of Wilton's right thigh with white-hot intensity.

Wilton grimaced and stumbled, but meeting a batch of recruits due to be sent out of the country within days was more important. He hobbled onward. No-one noticed the wound, which he tried to keep covered with his jacket while he briefed the young cadres. It was only when he stood to go to the toilet that someone noticed blood soaking his trousers and filling his shoe. Mkwayi calmly went outside to the toilet and drained the blood from his shoe.

At around midnight he left the meeting and limped to Ireen's house. She gave him painkillers and squeezed the wound until the bullet popped out. She had barely finished dressing the wound before Wilton fell into a deep sleep. The next morning he woke early to go about his work.

By late that afternoon his wound was throbbing with pain, and blood and pus filled the bandages. He returned to Ireen's house, where she cleaned and dressed his injury. They sat on the bed talking until late, making plans for their marriage later that year. Suddenly loud banging on the doors and windows of Ireen's two-room house disturbed the late-night silence. Mkwayi's name had long topped police most-wanted lists and they were about to tick it off.

Wilton had already been convicted in absentia in a trial with David Kitson, Laloo Chiba, Mac Maharaj and John Matthews, who were all sent to Robben Island after being convicted on charges relating to sabotage, membership of the ANC and the Suppression of Communism Act. The police were not only seeking Wilton; he had two brothers already serving time on Robben Island, and a third on the run as a fugitive.

With the absolute calm that comes from understanding destiny, Wilton answered the pounding by saying: 'The door is not locked.' He turned to Ireen and calmly said: 'The police have come to take me away.' The police burst into the house and found Wilton and Ireen sitting in bed.

'Who are you,' the police demanded.

'Who do you want,' Mkwayi countered.

'We are looking for Wilton Mkwayi.' They held up an old photograph of a much younger Mkwayi. The photograph bore little resemblance to the time-worn 41-year-old man on the bed.

He recalls today: 'I was stupid and said, "yes it is me".' Two policemen went out the house and whispered in Afrikaans to an unseen figure in a car. They nodded their heads and came back.

Wilton realised that the Judas was Tlhapane, his trusted comrade. Tlhapane later became a favoured anti-ANC witness for the state. He testified against his compatriots at the Rivonia Trial and later travelled to the United States to denounce the ANC before the Denton Commission. Much later, he and his wife were shot dead by unknown assassins. Mkwayi says: 'We were very sorry she died, she was a very good person. He never told her he was an informer.'

Ireen helped Wilton dress and gave him painkillers for his wound, then calmly opened the door for them all to leave. However, within minutes, another police team came in and detained her for three weeks. Her nine-year-old son, Sipho, woke in the morning to find his mother gone and neighbours caring for him. At Orlando police station the police opened curtains screening a window and ordered Wilton to stand there. 'I said: "Tell Tlhapane to come inside".' The shocked police whipped around and asked 'Who told you it was Tlhapane?' before realising their mistake.

Mkwayi sorts through the pencils on his desk, in a barren office on the 10th floor of ANC headquarters at Shell House, Johannesburg, as recollections intrude upon each other and interrupt his train of thought. 'Tlhapane was detained and released three times in 1963 and 1964. Unlike others he never showed evidence of bad torture. Some people became suspicious of him, but did not tell me when after his last release he went straight to the offices of the late Dan Tloome (later the chairman of the SACP), who was a bookkeeper.' (It was established practice that, after release, the security police would tail ex-detainees or prisoners. As a result no-one would visit people or places of consequence for days after their release.)

Now that the inevitable had happened Wilton's thoughts turned to marriage. During his trial, Wilton exasperated Joel Joffe, his defence lawyer, by asking if he could marry Ireen then. The defence team were more interested in keeping the noose from Mkwayi's neck than in helping him place a ring on Ireen's marriage finger. Ireen was 39, and Wilton 41; they never dreamed it would take another 25 years before their dream came true. Their quest seemed absolutely hopeless after Wilton was sent to Robben Island in June 1964. Wilton recalls, 'The island was a bad place in the beginning but we made it a place where we could sit and discuss, where we could study, some of us had never gone to school. I had only gone to school as far as Standard Four.' But on the Island prisoners won the right to study and Wilton managed to finish his schooling and qualify as a company secretary. He had nine credits toward a BCom under his belt when he was eventually released.

THE LONG QUEST

The indefatigible would-be bridegroom was no sooner settled in his cell than he made the first of 23 fruitless applications – one a year – to marry his beloved

Ireen. Prisoners, he was told each year, were not allowed to get married. Still he applied. After 20 years of applications the prison authorities finally asked social workers to dissuade Wilton from his futile quest. But they too were flummoxed. There was, they agreed, no law to say prisoners could not marry, but no-one could recall it ever happening before.

It took Wilton Mkwayi 16 years to be graded an A category prisoner. Before that, Ireen's twice-yearly visits were behind thick glass, grimy with the fingerprints of thousands of lost touches. Visitors sat on hard stools and spoke into crackly microphones. Before the end of the visit the warders would announce 'five more minutes'. There would be no further warning, and exactly five minutes later the screens would crash down and the microphone go dead.

But once he became an A category prisoner Wilton was allowed five visits a month. Contact visits began: he could finally feel her soft skin under his toil-hardened fingers. He would also trade letters for visits: 'Sometimes I would write two letters in November instead of five or six so that when my wife came I could see her more often, as many as four times a month. They would sometimes say the visiting list was full, but then I would ask for more time and sometimes see her for an hour and 20 minutes instead of the usual 40 minutes.'

Ireen retired from nursing in 1982 to enable her to visit Wilton each month, courtesy of the International Red Cross, which paid for her journeys to and from Robben Island. And then hope lifted: in June 1984, fellow Rivonia trialist Raymond Mhlaba married in an unusual ceremony arranged in top secret conditions by warder Christo Brand. Although Mhlaba was not allowed to have his beloved Dideka Letitia Heliso with him, he was accompanied by two 'best men', Nelson Mandela and Walter Sisulu. And so Raymond Mhlaba became the first political prisoner to marry while in prison. In June 1984, Mhlaba remained at Pollsmoor Prison while Dideka and his son Jongintshaba – acting as proxy – walked down the aisle at the Ascension Order of Ethiopia Church in New Brighton, Port Elizabeth.

Mhlaba, a widower, already had three children by Dideka, whom he had loved for 32 years. The grey-haired bride told journalists at her wedding that Mhlaba wrote to her in December 1983, asking her to marry him, and the two plotted how best to marry in defiance of prison rules.

By all accounts, it was a happy betrothal. The Right Reverend Dr Siqibo Dwane of Grahamstown, Bishop of the Order of Ethiopia, conducted the ceremony before hundreds of ululating, dancing New Brighton residents. Mhlaba's marriage lifted the spirits of others on the Island who were conducting romances by mail – and here Nelson Mandela's letters to his wife Winnie Madikizela are legendary – or through the visitors' grille, which is how Tokyo Sexwale met and fell in love with a young Afrikaans paralegal, Judy Moon, whom he married after his release in 1991.

THE WEDDING

In 1987, the prison authorities surrendered. Wilton Mkwayi lifts eyes rimmed with the milkiness of age, and recalls: 'It took us 23 years to be granted permission to get married. In June or July they said we could get married on October 30, 1987. The last day of October.'

There was great excitement in the cells that day. Before Wilton left for the mainland, his old friend and cellmate Elias Motsoaledi took him to the garden where he grew grapes, tomatoes and beans and, in between, calendula, marigolds, gypsophilia, everlastings and poppies. They cut a large bunch of flowers for the bride. Warders then led him to one of the new speedboats, *Penguijn*. It was foul, grey, gusty weather, and the boat thudded through the waves and sank sickeningly into the troughs of swells. The superstitious may have thought such bad weather carried an omen, but Wilton Mkwayi is not superstitious.

By 7 a.m. the excited bridegroom stood in his green prison clothes, holding Ireen's flowers, on windswept Quay Five of Cape Town harbour under the face of a blustery mountain and dared it to quench his joy. He was taken directly to Pollsmoor Prison. The head of the prison stood to greet him when Mkwayi walked into his office. Wilton asked, could he see his comrades at the prison, Nelson Mandela, Walter Sisulu and Andrew Mlangeni? The request was met with a firm 'no'.

Wilton's attorney had hired a suit for the elderly groom and he changed into these in the office. Black suit, white shirt, tie, black shoes. 'Ireen was wearing something whiteish with a big hat. Her sister, Mavis, who was her bridesmaid was wearing something similar.' The couple sat and had tea with their lawyer and the head of the prison. The warders then asked the couple to walk across the prison courtyard. Wilton and Ireen walked with dignity across the barren yard that formed their wedding aisle. While the two walked slowly along the concrete pathway, the sun broke through the clouds and sent beams of light to scatter the gusting grey mist whipping around the yard.

When they came back inside the warders told them, 'some of your comrades have seen you'. Nelson Mandela, Walter Sisulu, Andrew Mlangeni and others had silently crowded around their barred windows to bear witness to the greatest day in the life of Ireen Mhlongo and Wilton Mkwayi. The groom was 64 and his sweet bride 62 years old.

The two were ushered into a whitewashed room where they stood in front of the Reverend Patrick Matolangwe, a deputy to Anglican Archbishop Desmond Tutu. The groom stood tall, with only a slight stoop to his shoulders betraying his age. Ireen stood erect next to him, her hand cool in his palm. Four other friends stood outside. No prisoners were allowed to witness the ceremony. After the couple were pronounced man and wife they were allowed into a reception room where they had soft drinks. A prison photographer took a few photographs. Despite repeated requests Wilton never received copies of these, the only photographs ever taken of him with his love, and the author has been unable to trace them. A large wedding cake remained uncut. Ireen told him to share it with fellow inmates on Robben Island. As a special favour the bride and groom were allowed to spend three hours together. It was the longest time he had spent with her in 24 years.

After Wilton was placed in a prison van to be sent back to Robben Island, Ireen went to Cowley House, where the families of prisoners stayed before visiting inmates on the island. On that day, the house rang with singing and dancing celebrators, including a youthful, pretty Winnie Mandela in a curly wig and red polka dot frock, the always regal Caroline Motsoaledi, Philip Matthews, Cleophas Sibande and others.

On the Island, Section B was celebrating. 'When I came into my section the warders asked me to go to the hospital and kitchen to show the fellows there. They said if you go dressed as you are in your suit, the guards will think you

---

Ireen Mkwayi and Winnie Madikeizela-Mandela celebrate the first wedding of a political prisoner at Cowley House in Cape Town.

WILTON MKWAYI

are a church minister (and therefore able to move between sections without permission). When I knocked they opened the door and I went to the hospital and kitchen. The warders joked that no-one recognised me and I could walk to the docks ... ' As he tells this tale, Wilton Mkwayi is suffused with a gentle glow of pleasure: 'It is so difficult to describe how I felt. Not only I, but everyone in the prison was so happy.' The celebration was held in Section B and, in an unprecedented step, selected friends from sections G, E, F and A were allowed to attend. 'There were about 10 men from other sections, it was a very special day.' But tragedy had already whistled at Mkwayi's back as the speedboat returned him to the island from his bride.

'My wife must have been sick by the time we got married, but I never knew. She died on December 9, 1988. I came out of prison on October 15, 1989. One may say she was a coward to stomach all these things for all those years, and then when I was left with less than a year she decided to go.' He is angry, with her, with the prison authorities, with time lost.

But Ireen was not to know the decades of waiting were soon to be over. She was tired and cancer was consuming her body. Just before the first anniversary of their marriage she visited Wilton. It was an extraordinary visit, coming during the week and without notification. He was puzzled when warders called him for the visit. They had agreed to save up visits so she could visit him more often in December. She told him she thought she had cancer and that she was going to see a specialist who would tell him the diagnosis.

'But to my surprise, I was told nothing.' He must have had a premonition because, on October 28, he sat down and wrote his will, dividing the little he had between his three daughters, Tobeka Moss, Nosipho Moss and Tracy Toleko, as well as his eight grandchildren and Sipho Mhlongo, Ireen's son, and his son, Simphiwe (none of these children were the product of the union between he and Ireen).

'I received a notification from Johannesburg Hospital in November, saying she had had a successful operation. Then she wrote and said she had been operated on and felt better. She wrote again on December 1 and said she would be coming for Christmas but had to go to hospital beforehand for a checkup. I received her letter on December 9. The following day I was called by the major, he told me my wife had died the previous night, the night of the 9th. He said he had no details, a visitor would give me details the next day.' But all that was communicated to him was that people in Johannesburg wanted her buried on Heroes' Day, December 16. 'I said no, I wanted her buried on my birthday, December 17.'

Johannesburg's chief magistrate rejected this. The security police asked Wilton how many people might attend his funeral. He had been in jail for almost three decades; he had no way of knowing. He applied for a temporary release to bury his wife. The Robben Island prison authorities endorsed his application. But President P. W. Botha said no.

'His refusal was written in Afrikaans. I couldn't read Afrikaans. It was addressed to the colonel in charge of the Island who read it to me.' In the letter was a puzzling sentence. The State President said although he was refusing the application, certain steps regarding Wilton Mkwayi's release would be taken soon. Permission was given for Ireen Mkwayi to be buried on December 19, a weekday. Wilton Mkwayi sat in his cell and wept.

FREEDOM

Three months later, in March 1989, the prison authorities summoned Wilton and told him he was to be released from Diepkloof Prison, Johannesburg. It was the beginning of an extraordinary merry-go-round.

The day he left the Island, all the top brass of the prison lined the jetty to shake his hand and wish him well. At the mainland docks, however, there was confusion. The mainland warders insisted that Elias Motsoaledi should have also been released, but the Robben Island warders were equally adamant that no-one had given them such an instruction.

They placed Wilton's books and other belongings – three apple boxes, for a man who had lived more than three score years – into a van, and with two cars sped off to Paarl. The warders told him he would see Mandela in Paarl and Sisulu at Pollsmoor. 'Sisulu and you will go to Diepkloof tomorrow and be released. Motsoaledi should have been with you.'

'When we reached Mandela he asked where Elias was. He said the three of us were due for release.' The two men sat and chatted; they had not seen each other for six years. Mandela said that when Wilton was released he should go straight to Mandela's small old house in Orlando West to care for it until Mandela's release.

'Mandela didn't look much different, he is always trim, even in prison he did exercises every day between 4 a.m. and 6 a.m. After his release I warned his bodyguards that if they slept they would wake and find Mandela gone.' Mkwayi's eyes light up: 'Early in 1993 he was staying in his new house in Transkei and when the guards woke he wasn't there. When he came back three hours later there were 400 people looking for him. He had gone to look for the house of a relative and finally found it, but the neighbours soon came and in a short time 300 people were at the house talking to him.'

Wilton Mkwayi laughs, and then steers his thoughts back to that blustery day in March 1989 at Mandela's prison bungalow in Paarl. 'The phone was ringing and the Major who looked after Mandela answered it. He came back smiling broadly and said, "Mkwayi we will take you back later, you are going to Sisulu's place (Pollsmoor Prison), Kathi (Ahmed Kathrada) and the others must not see you. Tomorrow you and Sisulu will be released."'

A little while later the phone rang again and the major answered. Mandela commented: 'Look at that chap's face, he has bad news.' He returned and said: 'I don't know what to say, another office has said you must not see Sisulu. You are going to stay at Pollsmoor with Kathrada and Mlangeni.'

Later that day Sisulu was brought to see them for a few hours. The next day Elias Motsoaledi was brought off the Island to see Mandela before being sent back. The puzzled men asked a colonel at Pollsmoor what was happening. 'He said he believed SWAPO had passed a certain area in Namibia that they should not have, and now the government would not release us. We asked what we had to do with Namibia. But all he would say is that the department was saying that when we were released it would not be just three.'

It was clear, Mkwayi recalls, that the government had taken the decision to release them by December 1988, but were afraid. 'P. W. Botha was delaying things, so as soon as De Klerk came into power in September 1989, he said it must be done.' Other things changed too: the men received far more privileges, and when receiving visitors, had to wear civilian clothes, which were donated by a group of Cape Town businessmen. 'Even if we had a sports jacket and a nice shirt the warders would make us wear a tie, otherwise they would say we were not properly dressed.'

In September 1989, P. W. Botha, who had become increasingly erratic and an embarassment to the National Party, lost in elections to a hitherto undistinguished parliamentarian, Frederick Willem de Klerk. 'Between October 9 and 10, they came to us and said we will release seven of you, including Motsoaledi who was still on the Island. Mandela asked, "What about Jeff Masemola?" They said he is a PAC person.

But, Mandela said, "He has been in longer than us". They said they would consider it.'

Wilton Mkwayi and his comrades met with Mandela on October 10 and asked, 'Is it true you are refusing to be released?' He said, 'Yes, I am not going to let them release me now and you later. I told them to release you now and me later.'

They stayed with Mandela the whole day and had dinner with him at the prison time of 4 p.m. At 5 p.m., they were ushered out because Albertina Sisulu (Walter's wife) and Cyril Ramaphosa, leader of the National Union of Mineworkers, were due to call. The warders took the men on a tour of the prison grounds and let them visit the graveyard. They then went to the mess where the white warders ate. The warders said they had heard the men would be released the next day.

At midnight warders came to them and said 'Pack your things, you are being released'. But the prisoners were dressed and ready, their belongings neatly packed. They were told to go back to sleep and that they would be woken at 2:30 a.m. 'By 3:30 a.m. you must have finished bathing or showering. By 4:30 a.m. you must have finished breakfast and then we will go to D.F. Malan Airport.' By 5 a.m. a fleet of cars, one vehicle per prisoner, left the gates of Pollsmoor. Inside, flanked by warders, the prisoners in their brand-new suits and ties looked like chauffeured businessmen. A crisp breeze whipped through the pre-dawn streets as the first workers hurried on their way. The tall conifers of Tokai Forest seemed to lean down and watch as the fast motorcade swept away the night's final shadows and headed toward the rising sun and D.F. Malan Airport.

At the airport the men were ushered through a security entrance to a lounge where they were served tea and given morning newspapers. On the plane was a woman with a child, who gazed long and hard at these elderly African 'businessmen' accompanied by white businessmen wearing grey shoes (a dead public service giveaway in those days). The woman looked at Mkwayi and held eight fingers up. He nodded yes. The woman, a journalist, phoned in the news from Jan Smuts Airport in Johannesburg, and before the men reached Diepkloof Prison near Soweto, reports of their release were being relayed around the world.

As they drove through Johannesburg, they stared at an unfamiliar metropolis with its impressive highways and tall buildings. When the men went to jail, Africans were not allowed to walk on the same pavements as whites. Now they clogged the roads in hundreds of minibus taxis.

At 5:45 a.m. on October 15, the men were escorted home – with four carloads of security officials for each prisoner. The houses of Soweto had stayed depressingly familiar over nearly 30 years. Wilton Mkwayi was taken to Mandela's Orlando West home, where he found a group of people staying. Someone phoned Winnie Mandela, who was at the family home in Diepkloof. Cyril Ramaphosa arrived and told Wilton a rally had been arranged for that afternoon so the men could address the community.

On December 17, 1989, his birthday, Wilton had a tombstone erected for Ireen at her gravesite. It reads: 'Ireen Mkwayi, deeply mourned not only by her husband, Wilton, but by an entire nation for the work she did.'

POSTSCRIPT

But even when aged more than three score years, romance is possible. In 1990, Wilton began corresponding with an English nurse, Patricia Long, whom he

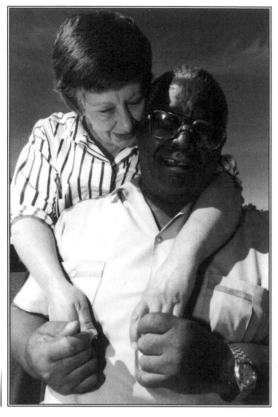

Wilton Mkwayi at the age of 73, took Patricia Long, an English nurse, as his bride on 6 April 1996.

THE ARGUS

met when he travelled to Britain after his release. By 1993, the relationship had deepened and in that year she travelled three times to visit him, and was at his side on his 70th birthday. Villagers in one rural area of the Ciskei were already petitioning for her to come and set up a clinic among them.

A small woman with a gentle demeanour, Patricia Long has a ready smile. A long-time anti-apartheid activist in London, she also has a deep appreciation of South Africa and its challenges.

'Do you think I am too old to get married?' Wilton Mkwayi asks. Clearly not, for at the age of 73, Wilton Mkwayi took Patricia Long as his bride, in a ceremony at Pelican Village, the parliamentary estate, on April 6, 1996. Wilton Mkwayi died on July 23, 2004.

The entrance to Robben Island, immediately after disembarkation from the ferry at Murray's Bay, was built of Malmesbury slate by political prisoners and painted with the badge of the prison service and the Robben Island lily emblem.

HEIN VON HÖRSTEN /SIL

COLLECTION TOKYO AND JUDY SEXWALE

1. *The main entrance to Robben Island prison with the warders' vehicles parked in front.*
2. *A camera smuggled to Robben Island prisoners by paralegal Judy Moon (later Judy Sexwale) in 1989 saw this picture of an unidentified prisoner, standing before the guard tower and fence, sent to the African National Congress (ANC) in exile in Lusaka, Zambia.*
3. *The Robben Island store was run for many years by unofficial Robben Island archivist and warder's wife, Desiree van Zyl.*
4. *Governor's House has long been used by visiting VIPs and statesmen.*

MARK WEDICOMBE

3

HEIN VON HÖRSTEN/SIL

4

HEIN VON HORSTEN/SIL

1. *The lighthouse was built in 1863.*

2. *One of the many wrecks that litter the Robben Island shore, or that lay around the Island beneath the waves.*

3. *The first black lighthouse keeper on the Island, Mr Jacobs began his work here in 1996.*

2

3

MARK WIDDICOMBE

HEIN VON HÖRSTEN/SIL

1 *and* **2.** *Two of the cemeteries on Robben Island – the bottom one was used exclusively for the burial of lepers.*

HEIN VON HORSTEN/SIL

MARK WIDDICOMBE

HEIN VON HORSTEN/SIL

3. *The leper church designed by Sir Herbert Baker fell into chronic disrepair over the years. It had no pews so lepers had to lie on the floor or stand.*

4. *The Anglican church has for more than a century served the 'free' inhabitants of the Island and is today a multi-denominational church.*

5. *The leper church lacked even adequate windows and in this instance had only a net preventing bats and birds from entering the church – which they still did to hang or nest from its rafters.*

1.   *Brenda Molefe pictured at Cowley House in Cape Town shortly before her marriage to a Robben Island prisoner.*

2.   *Ireen Mkwayi after her wedding to Wilton Mkwayi holding flowers plucked from the garden of Elias Motsoaledi on Robben Island by her groom; she is standing next to Caroline Motsoaledi, Elias' wife and Ireen's neighbour from Soweto.*

3.   *Tokyo Sexwale with a pen illustration of his eldest daughter. Drawn by a fellow prisoner and hung on his cell wall, this picture was taken with a camera smuggled into prison.*

4.   *An ebullient Judy Moon receives flowers garnered from the garden of Elias Motsoaledi and brought to her by a recently released Island prisoner in 1989.*

1

COLLECTION TOKYO AND JUDY SEXWALE

2

WILTON MKWAYI

3

4

ALAIN PROUST

MARK WIDDICOMBE

6

7

1-5. *Some of the wildlife species on the Island include tortoises, the indigenous Chukar partridge, indigenous mole snakes, seals and steenbok. Early sailors used to feed on seals, penguins and tortoises; the seals began to leave the Island to breed elsewhere and have still not returned in breeding colonies.*

6-7. *African penguins, once considered seriously endangered, are now thriving on Robben Island, due to a concerted conservation programme.*

1

2

HEIN VON HÖRSTEN/SIL

3

THE ARGUS

4

1. *These limestone quarries have been hewn for four centuries by generations of prisoners, but most particularly by the political prisoners incarcerated by the apartheid state.*

2. *The lepers' pool was believed to be therapeutic and healing to those lepers kept on the Island in the 19th century.*

3. *African political prisoners who worked in this quarry in the 20th century called the white plankton that accumulated on these rocks from the sea, 'the white scum from the sea', enjoying its dual meaning.*

4. *Nelson Mandela on a press visit to the Island shortly before his election as South Africa's first democratic president, chisels into a limestone rock for the benefit of cameramen. He is wearing dark glasses following an operation to his tear ducts damaged as a result of years of exposure to lime dust.*

HEIN VON HÖRSTEN/SIL

HEIN VON HÖRSTEN/SIL

1.   *A Second World War gun emplacement.*

2.   *An anti-aircraft gun from the Second World War.*

3.   *During the years following the Second World War gun emplacements on the Island
fell into decay and disrepair.*

4.   *Generations of schoolboys visited the Island even when it was used as a political prison
for camps in the quasi-military Voortrekker youth movement.*

3

4

1. *A ferry transports visitors regularly to Robben Island from the mainland.*
2. *An aerial view of the prison, showing the harbour in the background.*

THE 1960s:
YEARS OF TERROR

*Being life prisoners had one advantage, it is indefinite, so you
don't look forward to a date. Colleagues who had dates went
through a lot of mental suffering ... would they truly be freed? One
colleague was released after two years, immediately rearrested,
charged and brought back.*
AHMED KATHRADA

*If you are going to be a prisoner of your mind, the least you can do
is make sure it is well furnished.*
PETER USTINOV

Nelson Mandela stared out of his cell window, an arm leaning on the sill.
The sun, shimmering on the white sand, threw highlights onto his face.
The brief silence was interrupted by voices clamouring, 'Could we get some
emotion into this? A tear perhaps?' and 'Mr Mandela could you drop your chin
slightly?' or 'Mr Mandela could you drop your head in your hands?' It was
February 1994: two months later Nelson Mandela would become the first
democratically elected head of government in South Africa; now he was endur-
ing the media circus accompanying him to Robben Island to commemorate
the unbanning of the African National Congress (ANC) on February 2, 1990,
and his release from Victor Verster Prison nine days later.

Far away from Robben Island, amid the bleached farm land of the Free
State, then Pan Africanist Congress (PAC) deputy president, Johnson
Mlambo, was wiping his brow in the midst of a speech to a few hundred
supporters squatting under handkerchiefs and umbrella shades. His crooked
features – the result of having an eye gouged out on Robben Island – gave him
a fierce appearance that belied his gentle nature.

Limping slightly down a road flanked by vineyards, Christmas Tinto, a
genial grandfatherly figure, clutches a Bible and adjusts a dog-collar to imper-
sonate a priest – his cover to get onto a Cape wine farm and recruit the workers to a trade union.

All three men were close to achieving their lifetime goal: the liberation of
South Africans from apartheid and colonialism. The three had spent the better
part of their lives in prison. Nelson Mandela was in prison for 27 years.
Mlambo spent 20 years there, and was among the most brutally tortured of

Prisoners squat in the courtyard of the new maximum security prison at Robben Island, hammering stones into gravel for the Island roads.

Robben Island prisoners. Christmas Tinto spent so many years in jail and detention that he lost track of precisely how long.

In the early 1980s, when Johnson Mlambo was winging his way to Tanzania to form the PAC's military wing – the Azanian People's Liberation Army, successor to Poqo – Nelson Mandela was leaving the Island for Pollsmoor Prison and early clandestine negotiations with the government. Christmas Tinto was helping launch the United Democratic Front, the organisation that would raise the political temperature in South Africa to heights that made it impossible for government not to accede to demands for the unbanning of political organisations and the scheduling of democratic elections.

The political activism of Tinto and Mandela went back two decades before 1959, the year when Justice Minister Balthazar John Vorster (a prime minister 20 years later) designated Robben Island a maximum security prison for 'nonwhite' males. By that time, Tinto had been expelled from school for participating in a boycott; he led mine strikes as a worker; and, after seeing a woman with a baby chased by police seeking her pass, he joined the ANC and became one of its best organisers. Tinto was the first person arrested during the potato boycott and founded the railway workers union. Mandela was a founder of the ANC Youth League, together with Oliver Tambo. He led the 1950s Defiance Campaign and was a trialist during the four-year Treason Trial that began in 1956. By 1959 he was close to forming Umkhonto we Sizwe (MK), the ANC military wing.

Vorster was a hard, unsmiling man who fitted well into the cabinet of his dogmatic prime minister, Hendrik Verwoerd, the architect of apartheid. They believed that if blacks resisted plans to be merely 'hewers of wood and drawers of water', harsh measures should be taken. Robben Island was one of those measures designed to subjugate defiant black people.

The original Robben Island prison had 11 cells, but the huge influx of political prisoners in the early 1960s saw corrugated-iron structures erected, and prisoners sent to quarries to hew stone for the larger maximum security prison. Mornings would find condensation clustered on the walls and ceiling of the bitterly cold tin cells. It would drip onto prisoners' blankets, causing endemic respiratory illness.

June 13, 1964, when the Rivonia trialists arrived at the Island, was one such cold windy day. They had been taken from Pretoria Prison at 1 a.m., and under heavy security flown in a military aircraft to Robben Island. On arrival, they were graded D category, which allowed them one half-hour visit every six months and a letter twice a year of no more than 500 words. They had to perform hard labour, and for the next 14 years the prisoners hacked at the white walls of the huge ampitheatre of the lime quarry. They would return to their cells with blistered, bloody hands and sore muscles. Mandela and his cohorts

Mr Mejima, a prisoner in a Robben Island courtyard.

This political poster reflecting most of the Rivonia trialists – including Nelson Mandela, Ahmed Kathrada, Andrew Mlangeni and others – was typical of the latter phase of the resistance struggle.

were kept in single cells in Section B – reserved for top-ranking political offenders. Lower-ranking 'politicals' were thrown into communal cells with criminals and often subject to abuse.

For years they only had a Bible to read. It would take 26 years before Ahmed Kathrada, who went with Mandela on the first MK bombing mission to blow up pylons near Johannesburg, could describe in a carefully handwritten dissertation for a Bachelor of Arts degree the steps that led to black resistance: 'After 50 years of Union (1910), basic civil rights were still denied to Africans, coloureds and Indians. African rights to land ownership were restricted to less than 13% of the land. Passes, which only Africans were forced to carry (denied) freedom of movement and the freedom to sell their labour where they wished. Vast numbers of resettled people were uprooted from their homes and removed to areas demarcated for particular ethnic groups.

'African reserves had among the highest incidence of malnutrition, kwashiorkor and TB in the world. Over half the African population lived below the poverty datum line. Infant mortality was higher than in many poorer Third World countries.

'Vocal and active opponents of the regime were banned, banished and imprisoned. South Africa, in proportion to its population, had the largest number of prisoners in the world and the highest rate of executions – the overwhelming majority of them black.

'There emerged a picture of the monumental patience of the African people and their political leadership.

'Driven by nationalism, they aimed to win justice, human rights and liberty. For these they pleaded and petitioned ... to be met with rebuffs and increased inroads into their rights. In 1949, they turned to extra-parliamentary methods, in the hope that they would succeed in gaining the attention of those in authority. If anything, racialism became more brutal.

'The turning point in African political thinking came in 1961. African leaders took the first steps to move away from half a century of fruitless non-violent endeavour. ANC leaders found themselves with no alternative but to opt for armed resistance.'

RESISTANCE AND REPRESSION

The ANC formed Umkhonto we Sizwe in 1961, with Nelson Mandela as its Volunteer-in-Chief, to carry out acts of sabotage such as blowing up pylons and railway lines. Poqo, which Johnson Mlambo joined as a PAC member, adopted a strategy directed at killing whites or those seen as collaborators. The organisation grew rapidly. In 1963, Vorster introduced the General Laws

PHOTO KEY:

1. Watchtower.
2. Recreation Hall built for church services and film shows. At a later date, it was divided into three sections, namely a library, a shop and an activity room.
3. Kitchen.
4. A fence-lined corridor covered by barbed wire which leads to the quarry.
5. Sportsfield.
6. Main Communal Section. Each communal cell could hold between 50 and 60 prisoners.
7. Study Section.
8. Namibians' Block, where Namibian prisoners were held.
9. Library.
10. Hospital.
11. Solitary Block.
12. Tennis Court.
13. The Rivonia Group was kept here.
14. Prison Clinic which had 20 to 30 beds. A doctor from Cape Town visited the clinic twice a week.
15. Administration Block for the prison authorities.

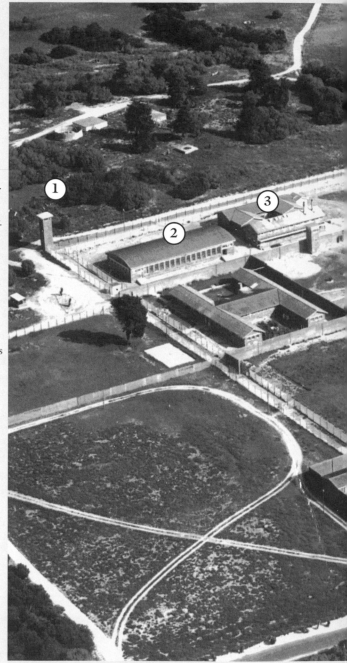

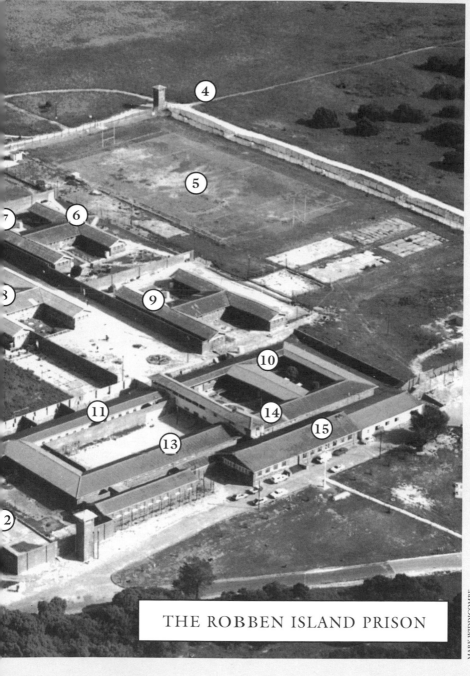

THE ROBBEN ISLAND PRISON

MARK WIDDICOMBE

Amendment (GLA) Bill, to permit detention without trial in solitary confinement for 90 days, which could be extended 'to this side of eternity,' he said.

One clause was directed against a single individual, Mangaliso Robert Sobukwe, leader of the PAC and Poqo. The GLA gave the Minister the power to detain political prisoners after they had served their sentences. On May 1, the law was passed. Two days later, Sobukwe, who was due to be freed after two years in jail, was transported to detention under the GLA on Robben Island. Police swooped on Poqo, detaining 3 246 of its members. By the end of 1963, 40 people had been sentenced to death and more than a thousand to sentences ranging from one to 25 years. By mid-1964, Vorster told Parliament that 202 Poqo members had been convicted of murder, 12 of attempted murder, 395 of sabotage, 126 of illegal departure from the country and 820 for belonging to an underground organisation, which Poqo had become.

This clampdown was seen through the eyes of a 10-year-old boy living in a Transkeian village. Sabelo Phama quietly herded goats for his father, a member of the local intelligentsia, and watched and listened as key ANC and PAC members visited his parents' home. He saw his parents' distress as, one by one, former visitors were jailed or executed. In the early 1990s, white South Africans shuddered when they heard the name Sabelo Phama, who became the feared commander of the the Azanian People's Liberation Army. APLA guerillas carried out attacks on white civilians in farming homesteads and golf clubs. Phama was a protege of Mlambo, and died in a car accident in Tanzania before the 1994 democratic elections.

In the 1960s, Dullah Omar was a young Cape Town lawyer, and member of the Unity Movement, who built a clientele around Robben Island prisoners. His first client was a man called Mapipa, a PAC member. Omar recalls: 'I regret my defence of him was unsuccesful, probably because I had only been practising for a year. In those first few years I acted for hundreds of PAC people. In the early years conditions on Robben Island were hell. It was terrible for prisoners, but even their lawyers were regarded as enemies. We would be insulted, shouted at, pushed around, and because we wanted continued access to our clients we tolerated it. Of course it impacted on me, there was a sense of outrage which lived with me all the time and I think helped shape my thinking about justice and the need for a new order in which the rights of people would be respected.'

Robert Sobukwe was one of his clients. Omar recalls him as a mild-mannered man kept in isolation on the Island in a small house set slightly away from the prison. Here, Sobukwe lived in excruciating loneliness until his release in 1969 to 12-hour house arrest in Kimberley, at a time when his body was already consumed by cancer, and death close by. On the Island, prisoners walking to and from the quarries would risk punishment by waving to him or

The prisoner identification card of Eddie Daniels. All black prisoners were issued with these cards on admittance to the Island.

singing to boost the spirits of the lone figure standing at a window. Liberal parliamentarian Helen Suzman visted Robben Island in February 1967, and met with Sobukwe, Mandela, Neville Alexander, Eddie Daniels and Laloo Chiba. She told newspapers that Sobukwe was 'beginning to be affected by the lengthy solitude'. Three years earlier his request for an exit permit – to leave South Africa with a vow never to return – had been refused.

REIGN OF TERROR

After the clampdown of 1963, African resistance became scattered and inef-fectual. MK was in disarray, with its High Command behind bars and other senior commanders in jail, exile or keeping a low profile and restrategising. The radical actions of Poqo and their attacks on white civilians made their members a target of Robben Island warders, and none were more cruel than the Kleynhans brothers – Jan, Evert and Piet.

When asked if he remembers any warders in particular, Christmas Tinto immediately says, 'Yes there were two lefthanded brothers, Piet and Evert Kleynhans'. He shakes his head and whistles, 'Those two, I wouldn't like to meet again, they were evil.

This sign to Section B shows the prison emblem of keys, a book and a scale of justice.

'If you had a headache and went to the hospital the doctor would ask what was wrong. Kleynhans would say, he's just come to see the hospital and would hit you on the head with his baton. The doctor would laugh and put a plaster over the blood,' he recalls.

Johnson Mlambo, who was a stocky 23-year-old when he arrived on the island, had particular cause to remember them. The Kleynhans brothers claimed that they read books on torture and that he was their favoured guinea pig. In some ways, though, Mlambo's torture began before the Island.

Arrested in March 1963 with seven others Abel Chilwane, Simon Nkosi, Josia Makofane, Nelson Nkumane, Michael Muendane, Lucas Mahlangu and Douglas Simelane – they had their first trial on charges of sabotage dismissed. But as the so-called Daveyton Eight walked out of court in Johannesburg they were re-arrested. With their legal funds depleted, their case fared badly without adequate defence counsel and they received lengthy sentences. Mlambo received 20 years.

It was Friday, June 21, 1963, when the men were convicted. The sun cast long, cold shadows over the small patches of lawn in front of the granite Supreme Court building as they were transferred to Pretoria Prison. At the prison, they were made to strip and run down a passage flanked by 12 policemen holding whips, who flayed them mercilessly before pushing them into icy showers. Three days later they were joined by nine men from Vlakfontein near Mamelodi, a Pretoria township. This group included some of the first men to be sentenced to life imprisonment in South Africa – Samuel Chibane, Philemon Tefu and Isaac Mthimunye, also Poqo cadres – and were put into the same cell as the Daveyton Eight.

The next day the men were handcuffed together in groups of two or three with what Mlambo calls 'automatic' handcuffs, which tighten and bite into the skin the more a prisoner moves. Mlambo was handcuffed between Ephraim

Bahula and Michael Muendane. They were put into the back of a prison van, with a lidless bucket to serve as a latrine. The men were given coffee and bread before they left at 4 a.m., and nothing more until they reached the Karoo village of Colesberg at 7 p.m. It was a long, uncomfortable journey on hard tin seats with the stench of urine and faeces and men sweating together in a fly-buzzing haze. At Colesberg Prison they were given food and shown to cells where they slept still handcuffed and wearing leg irons. Mlambo recalls, 'It meant that if one of us wanted to relieve himself, all three had to wake up and go'.

Late the next day they arrived in Cape Town and were made to lie on their stomachs in the hold of *Issie*, the ageing Robben Island ferry. On the Island, they were thrown off the vessel, their handcuffs making their wrists a bleeding mess.

The maximum security prison on the Island had just been completed and damp rose from the new concrete floors through the sisal mats that they would sleep on for the next 14 years. They soon learnt prison rules.

The walls of this corridor in the prison were paved with Malmesbury slate which was excavated by prisoners.

MARK WIDDICOMBE

African prisoners were given sandals, short pants and a canvas jacket, and were not allowed to wear socks or underwear, which Mandela says prisoners found 'very humiliating'. Indian and coloured prisoners, however, were also allowed shoes, socks, long trousers and jerseys. At weekends and on public holidays they were locked up for 24 hours, with 30 minutes exercise in the morning and the same later in the day. They were woken each day at 5:30 a.m. and had to be asleep by 8 p.m. – even though prison lights burned for 24 hours a day. At weekends they were locked up at 3:30 p.m., and at 4:30 p.m. on weekdays – with supper served half an hour beforehand. Despite doing heavy physical labour they could shower only twice a week, on Wednesday afternoons and Saturday mornings. They wore the same clothes all week until Saturday. In years to come, the Rivonia trialists formed a prison elite who were allowed to shower first. D category-entry level-prisoners were allowed to write and receive two letters a year. If they wrote to an 'undesirable' person the letter would not get posted. If the authorities did not like the content of a letter written by a prisoner, the offending passages were underlined and he was required to redate and rewrite the letter. If the prisoner refused because censorship of certain lines made the letter illogical, the letter was forfeited.

There were other deprivations. It was only in 1971 that African prisoners finally received bread. Non-African prisoners could not have puzamandla – powder mixed with water to make a sustaining drink. Mandela recalls that this drink was nourishing, but so much smuggling went on between kitchen staff and others that it was usually watery and tasteless.

Each day prisoners were searched. They had to strip naked, bend and touch their toes. A doctor would put on thick brown gloves, then put his middle finger deep into each man's rectum and twist it. Warders would beat men on the shoulders with pick handles if they did not bend low enough. Another variation was the tauza, where men would have to strip, leap across the yard and, as they landed, touch their toes for the humiliating medical ritual.

The first day for Mlambo and his compatriots set the tone for the next 20 years. They were forced to sing hymns and nursery rhymes while their heads were shaved. A hardened long-term criminal called Van Schalkwyk prowled around them, a finger occasionally shooting out to jab them, 'hello, my broers, vir wat is julle gevang?' ('hello, my brothers, what were you arrested for?') The men murmured they were PAC cadres. He asked how many years they had been sentenced to, then suddenly twisted around, his face creased with savagery and hissed, 'julle is nou by die Robben Island Congress, ons gaan julle ry hierso'. ('you are now at the Robben Island Congress, we are going to give you a hard time here')

The young PAC cadres were devastated to find threats coming from a man as brown as them. Mlambo and Philemon Tefu were sent with two other

One of the most famous of the clandestine pictures taken by prisoners on Robben Island and smuggled out shows Nelson Mandela and Walter Sisulu.

politicals to cell 6, in which 60 prisoners were crammed into a space meant for 20. There were four pails of water against one wall and another four used as toilets against the other. The stench was unbearable. Because water had to last the whole day, men rationed their water supplies – a mug full was all that was allowed for morning ablutions. Each man was given a mug, a wooden spoon, a tea towel to wipe dry his body and a toothbrush.

Sandals were placed in piles outside cells at night, and when the men were woken at 5:30 a.m., they were hurried out of the cell in the gloom, forced to grab any two sandals and quickly put them on. Often, the sandals would be too big or too small, or even be two left feet, but hesitation would meet with a beating. They had to walk with their hands straight above their heads or they would receive a sharp kidney chop in the sides from warders. 'We were forced to cower otherwise the warder would say, "kaffir, you are breathing on me" then he would assault us,' Mlambo recalls. The men would each take a wooden tray bearing cold soft porridge, soup and coffee and squat – they were not allowed to sit – in the yard while they ate. The Kleynhans brothers walked among the prisoners, rapping any whose buttocks touched the ground.

PROBLEMS OF NATIONAL STRUGGLE + CLASS STRUGGLE

National struggle and class struggle present a delicate problem in the struggle for liberation. These two demand well schooled minds both in Science

1. LABOUR Organization in our Revolution

The question of labour in our revolution has received special attention from the liberation movement. The movement has, in numerous statements and publications drawn the membership's attention to the fact that our national liberation/war is a socio-economic revolution. This is because S.A is a fully developed capitalist country. The working class has therefore to be fully mobilized. To mobilize this force trade unions become the most important mass organisation of the working class. The most politically advanced workers are recruited into the party of the National movement. Since many of us on leaving prison are absorbed in industry and commerce it becomes imperative that every one of us should have a good knowledge of trade unionism. There is much talk in government circles about new developments. Among these is the recognition of African trade unions by the government. In terms of the S. African law this means that African t'u's must be registered by the industrial registrar do that they could then enter into industrial agreements with the employers on wages and other working conditions.

The question may well arise as to why nationalist government has decided on this when the nationalist ideology doesn't countenance collective bargaining by the African workers? Has there been a change of heart? The heart of capitalism is profit and this profit is any the result of exploitation. So this heart never changes. The reason for this move must be sought in the revolution that is taking place in S.A. headed by the A.N.C, and the general decline and decay of capitalism throughout the world. It is a move calculated to isolate the w/class from the revolution and thus make it easy for the government to stem the tide of this revolution. The Nats government

... the African worker is reduced to the position of a serf under feudalism. Under all these conditions it becomes important to clearly understand both the African worker and the white worker. African workers come from the townships or locations, recruited and white farms. Their experience and work vary. What may constitute a basic need to an urban worker with a long life of urbanization may appear a fringe or marginal need to a rural worker, although today this is being rapidly reduced by the proletarianization of the rural area. The overwhelming majority of the white workers are, by and large, supporters of apartheid because i.e. tradition arising from the historical conditions of colonialism. If they talk of having African workers organized into trade unions this is paternalistic and aimed at containing the African worker so that he does not fall under left influence. We must, however, draw a sharp demarcation line between reactionarism and opportunism of the right and those gallant white revolutionaries who clearly grasped and applied the African international which transcends colour and race, from these the African worker will find true ally and comrade.

Workers enter industry still under all the influences of bourgeois class. Money and individual wealth, is still the thing to them, so we shall find flourishing 'banks' that lend out money on alarming weekly interests, getting clubs for race meetings, employers and so chapters despite all the talk about the recognition of African trades unionism among Africans is still more or less in matter of touch and go so must endeavour are hostile to African trade unions is, among other things, to weed out the moderates. As a result all this it became imperative to begin working the organization of units or cells in each workshop and also to organize such units to residential areas so as to contact them on their homes and their discussions out there.

Tight writing was typical of Mrabulo or political education documents.

Mlambo was put into the landbou span (agricultural team). He was given a pick and shovel and set off confidently. He was used to hard menial work and believed he could deal with anything that came his way. The men took turns carrying large barrels of food – usually boiled corn, sometimes with beans – to the worksite for lunch. At the site, they would remove their jackets and, within a short while, would be sweating with exertion. They were made to dig earth from the ground and cart it up a steep incline where they poured the contents of their wheelbarrows onto a growing mound that ultimately formed a small hillock. During the first days, huge blisters formed on their hands; these would pop and bleed, making their task a nightmare of deepening pain. Their legs and ankles could be lacerated by the strips of corrugated iron laid down to prevent the wheelbarrows from sinking into the mud. No first-aid treatment was available, so they applied urine to the wounds to sterilise and heal them. They were not given time off to relieve themselves and had to endure the humiliation of wetting their pants. Three weeks after building the first mountain of sand, they had to transfer it to another place, and so on, until the men felt their spirits slipping with every grain of sand that slid off the wheelbarrows. All the time the warders yelled: 'move fast, move fast'. Mlambo recalls beatings with batons and sticks torn from bushes.

'On one occasion as I was struggling to get up the hill, one of the Kleynhans brothers said to me, "you are struggling to get up, do you want to see a doctor?" I said yes. He said, "Lange, vat hom,"' (get him). A tall, mean convict, Lange grabbed Mlambo from behind, throttling him until Mlambo lost consciousness. When he regained consciousness, Mlambo staggered to his feet, still confused. The beatings immediately resumed: 'Work you lazy kaffir,' Kleynhans yelled.

There were never enough wheelbarrows. Some men struggled, their bodies bent close to the ground, hauling sacks of stones and sand to the dumping ground. Days dragged into weeks, with beatings, pain and the futility of their work demoralising the prisoners. One day Abel Chilwane broke down and sobbed while he was being forced up a steep incline with a full wheelbarrow. He said: 'With these insults and this work I am not prepared to go on, rather shoot me.' Evert Kleynhans called his older brother Piet, and said 'Piet, Piet, hoor wat hy sê. Hy sê ons moet hom skiet. Ons moet hom nie skiet nie, die Poqo, die kruiwa will hom skiet.' (We mustn't shoot this Poqo, the wheelbarrow will kill him.)

One day in late winter, Mlambo complained of exhaustion. The prisoners had spent hours digging sand and throwing it behind their backs, in a hard and fast rhythm, as the warders commanded: 'Skiet die grond ver.' (Throw the ground far.) Mlambo became dizzy, and Piet Kleynhans decided he would teach Mlambo a lesson. He got convicts to dig a deep hole, then threw

Mlambo into it and covered his body with earth but for his head. Mlambo was convinced he was going to be buried alive. He recalls no feeling of anger or fear, just a sense of hopeless inevitability. Even today he finds it difficult to talk about the incident. Piet Kleynhans stood before him and told Mlambo to open his mouth wide. Kleynhans unzipped his trousers and urinated in a long gushing stream over Mlambo. The other warders laughed; then Evert Kleynhans and a warder called Van Graan came to the urine-saturated Mlambo and yelled at him to climb out. As he battled to wrest his way out of the earth, he was beaten. Mlambo says that experience and others proved to him that the human being is much stronger 'than I ever thought. On another occasion I remember being struck with a pick handle on my neck and falling down. I remember thinking this is a delicate part of the body, I may not rise again.' While he was on the ground more blows rained on his buttocks and back. 'I rose and ran back to work.'

Eddie Daniels, who was jailed for his activities with the African Resistance Movement, describes Johnson Mlambo as one of the five most exceptional people on the Island. The others, he said, were Nelson Mandela, Ahmed Kathrada, Walter Sisulu and Neville Alexander. In his memoirs, Daniels wrote: 'Mlambo is an educated person and a gentleman, who refused to allow himself to be humiliated or degraded by the prison authorities. His responsible behaviour and courage set a good example.'

Mlambo said that during the 1960s stealing and smuggling of food from the kitchen was rife. The food was used to barter sexual favours from fellow prisoners. Mlambo disapproved, and one evening he confronted four prisoners who had stolen food. He was attacked and his eye gouged out with a sharpened spoon. Daniels recalls that on another occasion a warder claimed Mlambo threw soup across the warder's trousers, and sentenced Mlambo to six cuts with a sjambok. The other prisoners were working in the yard cutting stones. Finally, Mlambo appeared. He walked slowly across the yard. Silently and without expression, he sat on his brick seat, picked up his hammer and started to split stones.

It was Jean Amery, the French Resistance philosopher interned at Auschwitz by the Nazis, who wrote, 'those who are tortured remain tortured', and some become torturers. On a hot March day in 1964, warders handcuffed 12 prisoners, including Andrew Masondo – who would become a brutal torturer himself in the ANC prison camp at Quatro, Angola, in the early 1980s – and Bob Sogcwayi, while they worked, because they had protested their working conditions in the lime quarry. During lunch break the men were trussed to poles. They demanded to see the commanding officer. He did not come; after they were untied they were assaulted by prison warders in what warders called 'a carry on'. On another occasion Siva Pillay, an ANC prisoner, argued with a warder and was taken to the back of the sheds where he was hung by his hands all day. It was little wonder then, that Dr G. Hoffman, the Red Cross Delegate General, reported that Robben Island seemed grim, after he visited the Island in May 1964. No-one smiled, he said. Prison authorities told him there were four gangs on the Island and that there had been three deaths since 1963. One was a political prisoner who died from heart disease, one drowned while trying to escape, and another was shot while attacking another prisoner.

In 1967, the United Nations published *Apartheid and the Treatment of Prisoners in South Africa* which documented serious incidents of maltreatment. A public outcry ensued and newspapers reported that three warders had been dismissed and eleven transferred. The inquiry that led to the newspaper headlines had more dramatic ramifications on the Island than newspaper writers could have imagined. The Kleynhans brothers were called before a commission on the Island and questioned about the Mlambo incident, which was reported in the UN document. Two criminals known as Teeman and Bloed testified to the veracity of the Mlambo incident and others.

To understand what happened next, it is useful to know a little of the criminal life on the Island. Most criminals belonged to a prison gang, and there was particularly intense rivalry between the 28's and the Big 5's, who practised homosexuality and took 'wyfies' (wives) – usually young boys. A third gang, the Big 6, opposed sodomy. Some warders would, as jest, to punish other prisoners or to reward informers among the 28's or Big 5's, put heterosexual prisoners in the cells of the gangs, where they would be gang-raped. They tried this with political prisoners, but stopped after the politicals staged hunger strikes and work stoppages. Moses Dlamini, a former political prisoner, described one such incident in his book, *Moses Dlamini Prisoner No. 872/63*: 'One day Georgie, president of the Big 6, was kidnapped. After lockup, Jan Kleynhans and another warder went to Section A (a stone's throw from Mandela's quarters in Section B) and told him he was wanted at the office. They took him to the Zinktronk (steel jail) and locked him in the cell of the Big 5's, where Teeman (Kleynhans' lackey) and Bloed were staying.' He was raped repeatedly that night, his screams punctuating the night air, until he promised to become a wyfie and not go back to the Big 6. The Big 6 were shattered: they met the next day and dissolved their gang.

Against this background, the Kleynhans brothers learnt of the testimony of Bloed and Teeman. The next day they dragged them to the cell of the 28's. Terrifying cries could be heard as the men were repeatedly raped and assaulted. They were tosssed into the courtyard the next day, blood oozing from multiple stab wounds. Prisoners say they saw Jan Kleynhans the day after, with his head covered in bandages and his arm in a sling. Prisoners say he was beaten up by a senior officer for bringing disgrace to the Island.

CREATING A COMMUNITY

As his 20-year sentence dragged on, Mlambo realised that some of the most brutal warders softened their attitude toward prisoners as they became used to them. Study became a bond. In 1964, Mlambo and Dikgang Moseneke were among the first to be allowed to study on Robben Island. Moseneke went on to become the first black advocate admitted to the Pretoria bar, in the late 1980s, while Mlambo achieved his BCom degree.

As more prisoners studied, warders too started enrolling in courses. One named Delport, who wore the four downward-sloping stripes of the long-serving warder, had been among the prisoners' most brutal assailants. He was among those who, in 1964, tied the 12 to poles before beating them. In later years, though, he began studying, aided by Hector Ntshanyana, a teacher who had been sentenced to 25 years after a petrol bomb attack on a police charge office in King William's Town in April 1963. Ntshanyane helped Delport pass his junior certificate and then his matric. With education backing him, Delport was promoted to head warder, then superintendent, then chief warder. Mlambo recalls: 'When he was transferred from Robben Island in the mid-1970s he wept. He didn't want to part from his Poqos he said.'

Wilton Mkwayi recalls that the prisoners would try to build friendships not with friendly warders but with the harshest. Such a friendship would be worked on for months, usually out of sight of others, before the warder was encouraged to help with small things – a newspaper or a magazine, for instance. Warders who were outwardly hostile toward inmates were less likely to be suspected of smuggling than those who were sympathetic. In August 1964, the head warder at Robben Island, Jacobus Venter (46), was found guilty of trying to smuggle letters from jail for prisoners. Two were requests for money and another dealt with domestic matters.

But this did not stop smuggling. Later, warders became involved in more complex and dangerous efforts. By 1964, a precious radio had been obtained. In the years to come, some warders became vital conduits, carrying mail – including photographic negatives – from the ANC on the Island to the ANC in exile, and vice versa, through other couriers on the mainland. Mandela and Sisulu were among the first to realise that open hostility toward warders would only make matters worse. They worked hard at creating relationships. Mandela said some warders would say: '"Let's make sure they can never defy us again." but others would say, "people like these will do it again sooner or later. We should treat them like humans." The latter would have a kind thought for us every day and give us the feeling that we had friends among the warders. Ties of friendship still exist between us.' Indeed, Mandela invited three former warders to his inauguration on May 10, 1994.

Mandela and his cohorts worked hard to create a cohesive prison community with extensive links to the outside world. He refused to acquiesce to regulations that said complaints could only be voiced on behalf of individuals and not groups. Prisoners organised a grievance committee with representatives from various political organisations. The authorities vigorously resisted this at first, but finally allowed this committee to make representations to the Prisons Board with complaints and suggestions.

Mandela discouraged hostility toward the warders, and was courteous and dignified with them. His stoicism infuriated some warders, who found petty reasons to pick on him. They would claim he was not working hard enough. On more than one occasion, he and Walter Sisulu were put on a diet of rice gruel when it was claimed they had not toiled with the requisite energy. On another occasion, Mandela was made to strip naked and stand to attention for an hour in the cold cell.

When three judges – Judge Steyn, Judge Michael Corbett and Judge Grosskopf – paid a visit to the Island, they interviewed Mandela in the presence of Colonel Badenhorst, the notoriously mean-spirited commander of the prison at the time. Mandela complained about brutality, and the colonel threatened Mandela. The judges warned him not to make threats, and a few weeks later Badenhorst was transferred.

Prison cruelty was severe, but Mandela says their real enemy was within: 'the one who makes you ask yourself, did I make the right decision in leaving my family and letting my children grow up without security. Although I agonised over my family, I was still convinced that even if I had known how serious the consequence of my acts, I would have done the same.' That did not ease the emotional burden. One of the few times Mandela's carefully held composure ever betrays emotion is when he speaks of his mother. 'One of the saddest moments of my life in prison was the death of my mother. She was unschooled and up to the age of 9 she tried to send me to school. The acting king of the tribe then took me over, he sent me to school and treated me like his child. When I practised as a lawyer I tried to support my mother, but when I came to prison I could not.

'The last time she came to see me was in 1968, I could see she was not well. I watched her walk to the harbour and had the feeling I had seen her for the last time. She died later that year and I tried to get permission to bury her.' This was denied. 'The next shattering experience was the death of my eldest son in a car accident. He was not just a son but a friend. I was very hurt I could not pay my respects to him or my mother.

'There was also the harassment of my wife who lost her job at Baragwanath hospital as a social worker. She went from job to job. The police would come and say to the employer, get rid of this woman, they did the same to my children at school. But then Frank and Hirsch employed her and when she was detained for a year they paid her, when she was sent to Brandfort they continued to pay her.

'The warders used psychological persecution – whenever something happened to my family, I would come from the quarry and find a newspaper cutting on my desk.

'Wounds that cannot be seen are more painful than those that can be seen.'

Christmas Tinto was sensitive to Mandela's pain when his mother died. He took to the funeral the copy of *The Argus* newspaper, which carried the news that Mandela had been refused permission to attend the funeral of his mother in Transkei, and he read it out. 'I told them, your son was refused permission by the government to attend your funeral. On the day he came out of jail in 1990 he asked me to tell him about his mother's funeral. He said I must go with him and show him his mother's grave.' Because of ill-health Tinto never went with him, but it was one of the first things Mandela did after his release.

These symbolic words were carved into wet cement in the breakwater wall of the Robben Island harbour.

Tinto knew Mandela well, after repeated incarcerations (the first in 1963) on an island he first visited as a soccer player in 1956 – while it was still a military base. For six years, Tinto's fellow prisoners included other greats of the liberation struggle: Oscar Mpetha, Zoli Malindi, Muntain Qumbela, Bernard Huna, Melford Stuurman, Alton Feketshane, Cyril Gwija, George Ngqunge. Also in Section A with them were the other Rivonia trialists: the much-loved Walter Sisulu (the son of a domestic worker and a wealthy white building society managing director, who never directly acknowledged them, even in their one and only meeting when Walter was an adult, but paid for his son's upbringing); and Govan Mbeki, who devoted hours to penning precise recollections of the history of the liberation movement, squeezing two neatly written lines into every line of a notebook, which would then be disseminated to other sections, copied by scribes and studied in nightly political education classes. There was also Ahmed Kathrada, who Mandela described as a unifying force on the Island. Kathrada was put in charge of intelligence gathering and dissemination, together with Laloo Chiba and Mac Maharaj.

KEEPING INFORMED

A complex information cell network evolved and worked as follows: in each cell there were 20 or more prisoners. They were split into political 'cells' of three to five individuals. Cells were ultra-secret and people belonging to one cell would not know the identity of those in other cells. They would form a kolgas, or collective, and would pool money according to their means to buy goods for the collective cell. Each year the cell membership would change to prevent detection. (It also made it easier to track informers if cell members were at some stage betrayed.)

If there was a decision to be taken – for example, about a hunger strike – each cell would discuss the matter. A nominated member would give his cell's decision to a PRO (political sectional representative) who would collate all the information and report it to the section leader. Each of the seven section leaders (sections A, B, D, F, G, hospital and dining hall) would convey their information to another PRO, who would – as in a regional structure – convey it to the CC (a high organ in charge of political and general matters). In the 1980s this included people like Tokyo Sexwale.

The CC assimilated the information and passed it onto the CO (Central Organ), the equivalent of the ANC's external National Executive Committee. The CO included Elias Motsoaledi, Harry Gwala, Wilton Mkwayi, Govan Mbeki and Nelson Mandela. They would assess the recommendations and make a final decision which would be communicated to all.

These networks were very tight. If warders or others broke a cell, all the cells would immediately dissolve and reform with new members. This made life complex for kitchen staff, as each time they would have to learn the new codes for the different leaders, cells and sections in order to convey smuggled messages. Isolated as they were from other sections of the prison, it was imperative for the Rivonia trialists not only to have news from the world and South Africa, but to ensure they had political control over as much of the prison as possible.

Walls, guards, dogs, barbed wire, locked doors and distance separated the various prison sections. Smuggling became an art. Messages would be smuggled in scooped-out bread or slipped under a plate. At one stage so much toilet paper was being used as notepaper in smuggling that demand for supplies soared. Toilet paper was banned for a time until, in Section B, for example, Govan Mbeki – who no longer went to the quarry because of ill-health – was put in charge of the toilet paper. He was given a roll at a time, to dole out eight leaves in the morning and eight in the afternoon, so it could not be misused as notepaper. Kitchen staff were key information couriers, and it is not surprising that many banned tracts, sealed between layers of adhesive plastic, were buried near the kitchen. Prisoners would wait until no guards were in sight, then, in the shade of a large tree, they would whip out spades and bury Communist Party tracts, ANC literature and discussion documents pondering the war in Vietnam, the rise of the trade union movement, Marxism, Maoism and other illegal issues.

In later years, when prisoners were involved in productive work, painters were important couriers of information. Gates between all sections were open except for the gate leading to sections A, B and C. Prisoners would ask permission to go to the kitchen, or visit another section, and smuggle news. Those who found newspapers would throw three stones over the wall to another section. If it was answered with a similar rain of stones, the newspaper was thrown over. When prisoners received study material they would ask for adhesive covers, and a percentage of these would go to political commissars in the cells, who would keep them for cladding important documents. Today the archives of Mayibuye Centre at the University of the Western Cape preserve some of these sensitive documents sealed in plastic. The edges are grimy from sand and many hands, and the writing often difficult to read through pages thinned with age and constant use.

One 1969 document is typical of the time. Knowing that most warders would not read beyond the title, false titles were given: This one was headed 'Browlee's Introduction'. The contents are the 1969 ANC revolutionary programme, with ANC written as 'A...C' – indicative of the fear of the consequences should such documents be found. Such surreptitousness about titles and names for organisations fell away as the years went by and concealment improved. Information, particularly about other revolutions and the socialist bloc, was sought after. On one occasion, when prisoners were allowed access to the library, word got around that a particular book had interesting information on Vietnam. Prisoners queued to read it. The prison authorities decided it must be subversive if so much interest was shown in it, which is how President Dwight Eisenhower's *Mandate for Change* came to be banned.

Newspapers were not allowed for nearly 20 years. *Farmers Weekly* was the first magazine to be permitted and was the least censored – even *Reader's Digest* had chunks ripped out. When a prisoner, Dr Masala Pather, applied for magazines, newspapers and a radio, the latter two were refused. However, the prison authorities said that if he submitted a list of six magazines, one would be allowed. Mac Maharaj suggested *The Economist*, which was rejected by all the other prisoners. Finally, they agreed to make it one of the six, and to their astonishment *The Economist* was the magazine the authorities allowed. The prisoners were delighted, and for two blissful years they devoured each issue of the magazine. When Masala was released, Maharaj took over the subscription, ordering it air mail instead of surface mail. But one day a careless prisoner left a copy lying in a cell. A bored warder paged through it and realised it was packed with news. The next issue was censored so extensively that only the covers remained.

News about the outside world was such a thirst that prisoners risked being shot by crawling under fences to snatch a newspaper from a rubbish heap, or stealing them from the bags of priests, doctors and lawyers. Church sermons were never missed because it was not only a way for all prisoners to meet – and exchange news and smuggled notes – but many priests based their sermons on outside news events or would bring a newspaper, which prisoners would steal. Convicts who smuggled newspapers from the warders' homes were rewarded by political prisoners with a full box of Boxer tobacco for an English newspaper, and half a box for an Afrikaans paper.

PRISON LEADER

Towards the end of the 1960s, Mandela decided the prisoners' lot had to change. He drafted, with his co-accused, a document which they presented to the Minister of Justice on April 22, 1969. It was an articulate demand for their release, or, at the least, for their recognition as political prisoners. He wrote that he and his co-accused were kept in the single-cell section of the prison isolated from other prisoners. He cited by contrast, the prison treatement meted out to the Afrikaner political prisoners, Generals Christian de Wet, J. C. C. Kemp and others, charged with treason after the 1914 rebellion.

'Their case was in every respect more serious than ours,' Mandela wrote. 'Twelve thousand rebels took up arms. There were 322 casualties. Towns were occupied and considerable damage caused to government installations while claims for damage to private property amounted to R500 000. These acts of violence were committed by white men who enjoyed full political rights.

'They belonged to political parties that were legal, and had newspapers that could publicise their views. They were able to move freely up and down the country espousing their cause and rallying support for their ideas. They had no justification for resorting to violence.

'The leader of the Orange Free State rebels, De Wet, was sentenced to six year's imprisonment plus a fine of R4 000. Kemp received a sentence of seven years and a fine of R2 000. The rest were given lighter sentences. In spite of the gravity of their sentences, De Wet was released within six months and the rest within a year.'

Mandela pointed out that similar leniency was meted out to Second World War Nazi activist and Ossewabrandwag leader, Robey Liebrandt. 'The only way to avert disaster is not to keep the innocent in jail, but to pursue sane and enlightened policies.' No response ever came.

Fellow prisoners were in awe of Mandela. He was friendly but did not encourage familiarity. But he was fond of self-deprecating jokes. One of his favourites came from a time when he was working as a Johannesburg lawyer, and spotted a white woman having difficulty parking her car. Mandela helped guide her into the place. She offered him sixpence. He declined. 'Oh,' she exploded, 'you don't want sixpence, you want a shilling? Now I won't give you anything.' And off she flounced.

He was also compassionate toward fellow inmates. In the late 1960s Eddie Daniels became very ill; Mandela would come into his cell in the mornings and empty Daniels's toilet bucket and scrub it.

On first meeting Mandela, one is struck by his regal bearing. It is one of a person who knows he is born to greatness, but it is his charm and friendliness that inspires such warm feelings toward him. Perhaps few know the exceptional compassion that characterises one of the greatest men of the 20th century.

THE WARDERS

*Outside jail the enemy was remote, but inside jail the enemy
was there 24 hours. We dared not show any weakness in
front of the enemy, ...*
AHMED KATHRADA

*It was an act of unimaginable cruelty to place poor white,
unemployable male warders in charge of, in most cases,
extremely sensitive, basically law-abiding black prisoners with
aspirations toward human rights and freedom. It was an act of
unimaginable cruelty to us and them, ...*
NEVILLE ALEXANDER

Author's Note: The following chapter was written after interviews in 1993 and is written in that tense.

Magadalena 'Sissie' Cillie lived in Cape Town before she met her husband, Coenraad Cillie. He was one of the first warders at the new maximum security prison on Robben Island and, at weekends, would visit his sister, who lived next door to Magdalena's family.

One day he came looking for his sister and knocked on their door. Magdalena's mother told him his sister had gone away for the weekend and invited the shy young man in for tea. Magdalena helped her mother serve tea. She sat across the tea tray from the young man in an awkward silence punctuated only by her mother's questions to him. After that, Coenraad began calling at their home, too, on his weekends off.

Sissie never set foot on the Island until they were married in 1962. Coenraad had painted a picture of a little Eden, a beautiful island with 'lots of trees, flowers and animals'. He told her they would live in a lovely house with a garden.

The day of their marriage, Sissie and Coenraad left the wedding reception and, after a stomach-churning ride on *Issie* – the smoke-filled ferry that serviced the Island – they took a bus to their home. The bus stopped before a tiny ramshackle house. 'What hokkie is this?' she exclaimed, 'surely people don't live here?'

'Look in the windows,' Coenraad suggested. She did and exclaimed, 'Why is my furniture in there?'

'It's your house,' Coenraad responded. Sissie began to cry.

They opened the door and stepped in. There was a lounge, a kitchen and a bedroom; the toilet was outside, with a washbasin, and an ugly big coal stove dominated the kitchen. When she turned on the tap, brackish sea water glugged out. She sobbed next to the faucet.

'For the first two years I wanted to run away, I bathed in sea water, washed my hair in it, we did everything in sea water. It is only in the last two years (since 1991) that we have had fresh water.' After she had been on the Island for two years, one day she packed her bags, and marched down to the harbour with her husband patiently following. When she reached the dock she burst into tears and returned home.

There were frequent electricity failures and Sissie kept a supply of paal kerse (large candles) to light her home. 'In those days there were only four bus stops on the Island, not like today where the bus will stop at each house. I used to sometimes wait in the rain and wind with my child.'

Travelling to and from the Island necessitated a trip aboard the venerable *Issie*. The vessel had only a few benches, which were ignored in favour of a position on deck in order to escape the smells of fresh meat, oil and fish that belched from the hold. The boat would dock at Quay Five, in the same place that the Island ferries dock today. While this mooring is alive today with the fashionable restaurants and shopping areas of the Victoria and Alfred Waterfront, in those days it was a vast grubby quay. Sissie would hoist her bags, take her child's hand and walk two kilometres up a hill to the buttressed sur rounds of the old Somerset Hospital and from there take a bus into town. In later years, she kept a car at the Wynyard Fort.

In time, Sissie grew to love the Island: 'You are free on the island.' But 'freedom' had a price. In winter, when the sea was choppy, the ferry would not run for days. 'It's not like living in the city, everything has to be planned. I could not just pop out from work at lunchtime to get my hair cut or do a quick bit of shopping. Working women had to wait for the weekend. I used to make a list and calculate the amount of time I would spend at each place to ensure I returned to the ferry on time.'

Her husband loves the Island, and, like many of the warders, would shed his uniform after work and head for his fishing boat.

Sissie regrets never having a garden. 'I'd live here forever if I could grow flowers,' she says wistfully. The shortage of water was so acute on the Island that warders were forbidden from keeping gardens and only a few tubs of flowers survived on recycled bath water. The warders' homes were dull little pink-, blue- and apricot-hued boxes sitting on tracts of khaki-coloured scrubland. Sissie is grateful that her only child, Correne (who also worked for Correctional Services before leaving the Island to marry and have twins) grew up with the myriad adventures and freedom that only Island children had.

ISLAND SCANDALS

By 1993 – the time of this interview – Sissie and her husband had lived on the Island longer than anyone else. She knew all the gossip that she cared to tell, which was not much.

Affairs – between warders and other wives, or even between prisoners and warders' wives – dominated Island gossip. Prisoners who exhibited good conduct and were not considered dangerous were allowed to work in senior warders' homes as servants or 'monitors' if they passed medical tests showing they had no diseases such as tuberculosis.

On one occasion, a prisoner was taken to the hospital with a bullet wound. Other prisoners whispered that the man had been having an affair with the wife of a warder, who came home, found them in bed together and extracted his revenge. It is not certain if this is the same as an incident Sissie recalls, about a neighbour whose hair she used to style. One day the woman's husband came home and caught the servant raping his wife. The man fled into the bushes and warders went after him with dogs. 'There were two men fishing on the rocks and he ran toward them (realising the other warders would not shoot for fear of hitting their colleagues), they tried to jump across the rocks away from him and one fell and broke his knee.' She says warders caught up with the fugitive who in the struggle she says, seized a firearm 'and shot himself in the mouth'.

Desiree van Zyl, who ran the Island store and meticulously compiled memorabilia and press cuttings about the Island over many years, remembers another incident. Van Zyl is touching in her need to communicate Island lore. She has kept folders, files and photograph albums for years, and loves to share her knowledge – while her daughter disappears next door to bake an apple tart for the visitor because Desiree's oven is broken.

Desiree sits at her neat dining room table and smooths the nylon lace tablecloth. 'The woman's husband was away doing a course, he was either a captain or a major.' A prisoner managed to evade evening roll call and prison authorities did not realise he was not in his cell but under the bed of the absent officer's wife. As she climbed into bed after putting her children to sleep the man clambered out and raped her. 'She had to keep quiet for the children. Heaven knows what she went through, some say she was half-mad afterward.'

Sissie remembers the rape, too, of a teacher who lived on her own in a small house near the jetty. The man involved in that incident received the death sentence. There was yet another incident, in 1966, when the wife of a young warder called Van Niekerk was caught having sex with a well-built 26-year-old prisoner from Krugersdorp called Biza. He had worked for some time in the Van Niekerk household and prison lore had it that he and Mrs Van Niekerk carried on a passionate three-month affair.

Warders used dilapidated vehicles such as this one to ferry themselves and their families around Robben Island.

During this time, the insatiable Mrs Van Niekerk told Biza she needed to disguise her affair with him by having an affair with a head warder called Lamprecht. On the day in question, Lampies arrived unexpectedly to visit his mistress and heard sounds coming from the bedroom. There was the muscled prisoner on top of Mrs Van Niekerk, who had her legs wrapped around him. Lampies closed the door quietly and scuttled off to tell his superiors, but Biza had seen him and by the time Lampies arrived back with the commanding officer and another senior officer, Biza was scrubbing the floor, and Mrs Van Niekerk demurely reading a novel. The Island authorities were in a quandary: Mrs Van Niekerk hotly denied the allegations and they in turn did not want a scandal. The prisoner was put on a spare diet and relieved of his floor-scrubbing duties.

Moses Dlamini also writes of this incident. He says that, afterward, when common-law prisoners had to strip for a search, the prisoners and warders noted Van Niekerk watching Biza closely. 'When he saw him naked, he let out a sound 'Meeah' like a goat. Everyone laughed.'

After the incident the plump Venus seemed singularly dissatisfied with the new monitors sent to assist her. Dlamini says the convicts discussed this, 'and decided the woman wanted to have sex. The incumbent was told to go back, greet her nicely and pat her buttocks. The next day he reported that he did that. She said: "You clever boy," and led him to the bedroom. When the husband came for lunch she said the new house servant was obedient and hard-working, and he could stay.'

PRISONER AND WARDER

The most common interpersonal relationships on the Island were not of a sexual nature, however, and developed between prisoner and warder. Close relationships grew over time. It was no coincidence that Nelson Mandela invited former warders, Lieutenant James Gregory and prison chef Jack Swart to his inauguration as President and toasted them by name.

In reminiscing about prison, he sometimes makes mention of the officer in charge of Victor Verster Prison, Major Marais, and of Lieutenant James Gregory. The two were bound in later years by the loss of their sons in (separate) car accidents. It was Lieutenant Gregory who had to break the news to Mandela that his son, Tembekile, had died in a car crash. Gregory recalls that Mandela's face froze, he turned on his heel and walked away. Other warders told him Mandela did not sleep for the next few nights. He stood at his window staring out at the vague smudgy lights of Cape Town.

'I only realised what he must have been thinking and how he felt when I lost my own son 20 years later,' Gregory recalled.

Saths Cooper remembers, 'Sometimes you would look at the things these guys (the warders) were doing to you and it was just fear, fear of the unknown. Some really believed a great army of revolutionaries would come from the north to free everyone.'

No army came. Instead, in April 1994, South African voters elected as President the man who made Robben Island a historical treasure – Nelson Mandela. On May 24, 1994 at the first joint sitting of Parliament following his inauguration, President Mandela told the country: 'The time will come when our nation will honour the memory of all the sons, the daughters, the mothers, the fathers, the youth and the children who, by their thoughts and deeds, gave us the right to assert with pride that we are South Africans, that we are Africans, and that we are citizens of the world.

'Our single most important challenge is to establish a social order in which the freedom of the individual will truly mean the individual – the liberation of the woman, the emancipation of the man and the liberty of the child.' And a former prisoner set South Africans free from the prison of apartheid.

ABOVE: *The interior of a cubicle at which prisoners sat to view their visitors and speak to them over a phone.*

ABOVE: *Christo Brand, pictured here with Nelson Mandela and Graça Machel, was 18 years old when he was sent, as prison warder, to Robben Island in 1978. 'I was told these were the biggest criminals in history and was quite frightened,' he said. Over time, Brand developed close relationships with the political prisoners, in particular Mandela. He was transferred to Pollsmoor Prison in 1982 with Mandela and a handful of the Rivonia trialists. In 1985, when his son Riaan was 18 months old, Brand defied prison rules and took the child to meet Mandela. Political prisoners said the thing they missed most was children. A warder motivated by kindness, Brand mailed letters for Mandela and bought him little treats, like his favourite hair oil, and even arranged for him to go on the occasional weekend trip out of prison. Mandela still calls him on occasion, and invites him to lunches and celebrations.*

THE 1970s:
YEARS OF STRUGGLE

*'From every dead child a rifle with eyes, and from every
crime bullets are born which will one day find
the bull's eye of your hearts.'*

PABLO NERUDA, *'I'M EXPLAINING A FEW THINGS'*

Christmas Tinto was a grandfatherly man with a face crinkled by smiles. He had the dignity and old world manners of people like Nelson Mandela and Walter Sisulu. And he was one of the few political prisoners to have been jailed on Robben Island more than once.

On a cold Cape Town morning in 1971, his family was woken at 2 a.m. by loud banging, and found their home encircled by security policemen. With his wife and children crying, Tinto was led away: 'I had a feeling I might never see them again.' He was put in a freshly painted cell; the policemen said the previous occupant had hanged himself. A fellow prisoner, however, said the previous occupant had been beaten to death and the walls painted to cover the blood. 'I couldn't sleep, I sat on the blankets all night,' Tinto recalled.

The next day, four security policemen – whom he remembers as Spyker van Wyk, Steenkamp, Swart and another – came to fetch him. They took him to a hall and told him to strip, 'I left my underpants on. I was told to stand on top of a chair. They took chains and some wires and put them over the rafters. They handcuffed me and hooked the handcuffs to the chains, they kicked away the chair and took off my underpants. They put a cloth bag, like those bags that you take money to the bank, but bigger, over my head.

'Do you remember those old telephone exchanges that you put clips in? They put clips like those on a battery, then plugged it into the wall. They took the iron clips and attached them to my ears and feet. I was hanging there, blood pouring down my arms where the handcuffs were cutting into them. An electric shock was applied ... they said: "Tinto, tell us, who is your contact in Johannesburg" – I was involved in recruiting for MK. I said, "Okay I am going to tell you." They took off the clips and let me stand on the chair. I said, "Gentlemen, I know nothing, I said that because this is hurting." They said, "Jy praat kak, kaffir." (You're talking shit, kaffir.)

'This time they pulled out my nails one by one – "praat, praat, praat" (speak, speak, speak). They held my genitals with pliers, it was a terrible experience. I thought, they are going to kill me. I lost consciousness. On the third week I awoke in a bed at Valkenberg Mental Hospital, tied with a white rope, hands and feet. I saw a doctor standing near my bed. I asked him "Is this Pinelands station?" He looked past me at another doctor and said, "He is alright." They told me I was brought by security police and said the police had told them how I had been tortured and that I had written a statement. I couldn't remember any statement. When I stood up I became dizzy. I stayed in hospital another two months.'

After that he was taken to court, where he was defended by Dullah Omar. 'In court was a woman with Dullah. I asked "Who is this person?" My wife cried. The police had long ago told her, "Christmas has passed away, he has killed himself."' Tinto was subsequently sentenced to seven years on Robben Island for recruiting cadres for Umkhonto we Sizwe (MK), the ANC army. Two years later he was released on appeal.

In 1992, following the unbanning of the ANC, Tinto saw Steenkamp at a function. 'He came to me and held out his hand. I hesitated to give him my hand. I said, "Are you being honest?" He said, "Yes Mr Tinto." I took his hand. He held my hand for a long time and reminded me that the ANC had asked everyone to reconcile.'

After his release from jail in 1973, Tinto was detained on five more occasions over the next decade while helping build the United Democratic Front (UDF) with people like Oscar Mpetha, Zoli Malindi, Trevor Manuel, Cheryl Carolus, Johnny Issel and Mildred Leasia. The late Oscar Mpetha became the UDF's first president at its launch in 1983, and Tinto its vice-president. By 1984, Mpetha's health was deteriorating and Tinto became UDF president. More than anything, the UDF grew out of the 1976 Soweto youth uprising.

CLASH OF GENERATIONS

It was that uprising and the events leading to it that saw the biggest and most militant influx of political prisoners onto the Island. Most of these youth subscribed to the aims of the Black Consciousness Movement (BCM). So angry and radical were these youth that they threatened the hard-won gains of older prisoners (such as access to books or study privileges) and, on occasion, conflict erupted between older and younger prisoners.

By the late 1960s and early 1970s, many older prisoners had adjusted to their isolation, and the exiled liberation movements had become but a vague dream. However, far from the Island, history had intervened when a shipload of African-American students berthed briefly in Durban in 1969, and discussed the works of seminal US civil rights leaders like Malcolm X (whose written works were banned in South Africa) with students like Steven Bantu Biko, a

Nelson Mandela's cell as photographed during a visit by journalists in 1979.

young medical student in Durban. The Black Consciousness Movement would later be born under Biko – who was murdered in jail in 1977 by police officers.

Nelson Mandela found that the respect he enjoyed among older prisoners was not always shared by the new inmates. On one occasion a young prisoner from Atteridgeville, Ronnie Mamoepa ran up a prison corridor and leapt on to Mandela's back, to show that he was human, too. Mandela was not amused. Mampoepa subsequently joined the African National Congress and has for many years been the spokesperson for the Minister of Foreign Affairs.

Clashes between prisoners and warders became commonplace. The youth of 1976 were not prepared to tolerate racism or insults from warders. In May 1979, six young prisoners were charged with attempting to kill Captain K. Harding, second in command at the prison. Harding later told a court that on February 9, at 8 p.m., he found 29-year-old Khumbele Mnikina addressing a group of fellow prisoners – Usumzi Mcongo (19), Zuko Camaqu (18), Mncedisis Siswana (22), Tamsanqa Jeffery Klaas (22) and Fezile Lawrence Mavundla (20). Harding ordered them back to their cells but they refused. He said the prisoners shoved him backwards through the gate. Mnikina held Harding by the throat and pushed him against the wall. Someone stabbed his left wrist. Harding wriggled away and fled. Mnikina threw a brick at him. As stones rained after him, Harding yelled, 'You will hang for this!' Prison warders were terrified by this incident, and the result was increased repression. But the youth felt what older prisoner Mac Maharaj expressed years later: 'The most punishing thing about prison was coming from the heat of battle to accept that you are on the sidelines.'

Among the post-1976 prisoners, there was also a strong anti-white element. In 1979 this led to fighting in the cells, and a number of ANC people (who believed in non-racialism) were stabbed. The culprits were arrested. Nelson Mandela, who witnessed the incident, refused to give evidence. Other ANC members followed suit. The case was dropped, and this increased the younger prisoners' respect for the ANC.

Despite these tensions, the Island was safer than jails on the mainland. Both Xolani Yengeni and Arden Bosman, 17 and 14, respectively, when they were jailed on the Island, witnessed the rape of young boys in mainland prisons before arriving to the strict internal discipline of the Island prisoners. Politics were also a barely learnt skill, for many late 1970s youth, and the ANC and PAC were half-forgotten organisations. PAC and ANC recruiters would meet them in jail and ask their affiliation, and more than one answered 'CNA' (the name of a mainland stationery chain).

Not all arrived on the Island because of political commitment, either, the late Andrew Mapheto recalled. Some were arrested while burning, looting or stone-throwing and, in the paranoia of the time, had serious political charges levelled against them. Recruiters would try and encourage political affiliation by gifts of soap, tobacco and kindness. The ANC argued for dual membership of the PAC or ANC with the BCM. Walter Sisulu's daughter, Lindiwe, and Winnie Mandela, then wife of Nelson, had both belonged to BCM structures while retaining a commitment to the ANC. The ANC also argued that short-term prisoners would be in danger of arrest on leaving the Island if they showed overt commitment in jail – where guards monitored them – to either the ANC or PAC as banned organisations.

Prison authorities tried to create conflict by placing different groupings together. Instead, Mandela said, 'it was an advantage, we could now start a debate on matters of unity. We were also able to assess the mistakes make in political activities and plan for the future.'

Saths Cooper, a former BCM leader, said in later years, 'The island has been so romanticised people have tended to reduce the dark hours'. Small things would heighten a sense of isolation and confinement. The windows, he recalled, 'were like ordinary windows with double panes – one sealed and one that could open. When we arrived at the island two days before Christmas in 1976, the part that could be opened was soldered. The windows on the passage side and the back wall were small prison windows with 2-inch water pipes instead of prison bars. The slightest touch to the bars would reverberate throughout the prison.' Prisoners would preface announcements by banging the bars with spoons.

Cooper said most new prisoners 'were illiterate, so guys liked Eric Molobi began teaching people. You don't know what joy it was when someone who was previously illiterate showed you a letter they had written. Some people didn't even understand the time implied by their prison sentences, we had to show them using string. The 1976 new intake also injected new lifeblood; they could tell stories of people outside, what women were wearing, the latest music, all sorts of things.'

EDUCATION

In fact, education classes had begun some years earlier when prisoners began coaching other prisoners. Mandela told inmates it was imperative they improve their education and prepare to govern. He set the example by continuing his studies by correspondence through the University of London. Curtailment of study privileges became one of the worst punishments a prisoner could receive. Neville Alexander recalls that on one occasion a prisoner in the general section wrote notes in ballpoint on his hand about matters he wished to discuss with a visitor. A warder saw this and the prisoner was denied study privileges for three years.

The prisoner tutors were tough. Archives show that J. Goabenie, writing examiner's comments in March 1973 for English exams, wrote that prisoners should be forced to speak English in class. Describing, 'the Attitude of Students toward Teachers' he wrote: 'It is a fact that our students are lazy. They do not do their homework. This is shown by the mistakes committed in their grammar.' An unnamed high school examiner, also a prisoner, complained: 'students are generally slow, about three-quarters answered only four of nine questions. Students are not keen and deligent [sic] in/on their work. Lack of confidence: In most cases, there are lots and lots of cancellations and mostly, correct answers are replaced with faulty ones.

'The language used by our students is frigid. It is wan of any devices and embellishments. Only one student used one simile and the other faultily used an idiom. Another student is suffering from what I may term as megalomania of pomposity, wasting time on self-inflation. Of the 29 students who wrote JC English (10th grade) only six were up to standard.'

Robben Island
Po Bo.
Robben Island

Robben _____ra Ndyolo   Roto
Robben Island
Pa. Bo.
Robben Island

MR dick Plase give me testimoal.og rethmetic, beCause I must
Oolong Prectise, the periot to the end of the year; so that
in the beginning of the nexst year, to be clar beal.
I feel that is neesisary, because I have enofe time to do it
ef I wait util umtil nexst ejeur The athers will be
from me to far, and it will tak long time.
befor I reech ther stage, and with out that, I feel hurry
For the rethmetic, because my work out side I am
Brick lar, and that work meds megement, I will be
plased if you think about It, and feel with me
I receve my letter yours fethful Richard N ydole

*Education was the most important activity on the Island. Most prisoners had received no
formal education and were taught by fellow prisoners.*

Prisoners had to sign a document saying they would not use study materials for purposes other than learning. Books, other than study materials, had to be ordered from the 'non-European' section of the State Library in Pretoria. Prisoner B. Konile expressed the despair of most when he wrote, 'land is gone, cattle and sheep are not there any more. What's left? Learning ... I want the shield and spear of learning.'

Prisoners would return from the quarries or their work at 4 p.m. and, within an hour, would settle down for an intense period of lecture, debate, criticism and insight into subjects as diverse as history, geography, politics, philosophy and anthropology. This process was called Mrabulo, and drew on the

single cells xmas knockout competition
robben island

★

presented to

winners of the tenniquoit championship

e.j.daniels   .   r.c.wilcox

BY THE SINGLE CELLS SPORTS CLUB

[signature] .... CHAIRMAN

E. J. Daniels.

M. S. Essop.

26 TH DECEMBER, 1974

MAYIBUYE CENTRE

Prisoners gifted in calligraphy would make elaborate certificates for recreational awards.

work of writers as diverse as Plato, Marx, Brian Bunting, Joe Slovo, Dan Tloome, Robert McNamara, Joshua Nkomo, Mao Tse-Tung, Alexis de Tocqueville and Bertolt Brecht, as well as smuggled articles from the Encyclopedia Britannica and from newspapers such as *The New York Times* and the *Cape Times*.

A typical programme would be like that followed in Section C at that time: Monday to Wednesday, philosophy would be studied from 5 p.m. to 6:30 p.m., and on Thursday and Friday prisoners pondered the strategy and tactics of the ANC. From 7 p.m. to 8 p.m., they examined the history of the ANC, and this would include debates on the Freedom Charter, ANC constitutional guidelines, the rise of the proletariat in South Africa, the history of the South African Communist Party, the Comintern and the black diaspora. Up to 43 subjects could be included, and each would necessitate careful research by selected individuals, who would write out by hand their arguments for reading and analysis not only by their cell members, but by those in other cells and sections of the prison. Discussion documents would be carefully concealed in loaves of bread, buried with plastic covers under a tree near the kitchen for later retrieval or thrown over walls after a certain number of stones were thrown over to ensure no guards were around on the other side.

While censorship on the mainland was rigid, and books or documents about communism or socialism could only be obtained with special permission for students of politics at university libraries and then read only on the premises, Robben Island had probably the country's greatest selection of communist and socialist literature, most of it smuggled in. Jailed MK cadres would write down what they recalled from their studies in the Eastern Bloc. Lenin and Marx would have wept with gratitude. Some of this literature was extremely obscure: prisoners studied treatises, for example, on Vietnam, which included the country's entire constitution – article by article. At one stage the leadership instructed each section to take a continent and study it in depth and prepare reports for other sections. Little wonder then, that even today men from the Island can still quote line by line, page by page, words from certain books, speeches and debates.

There was an obsession with acquiring knowledge to help build a new way for South Africa. Little wonder then that school boycotts, although viewed as a necessary part of the struggle for freedom, should have caused so much pain to Nelson Mandela and Walter Sisulu when they left prison and found a youth ignorant of how knowledge could transform and mould people.

A NEW REGIME

From 1966, prisoners on the Island enjoyed a relatively enlightened period of governorship by the warders, but a more repressive climate developed between 1970 and 1972, coinciding with a more radical phase of the political struggle on the mainland.

In late May 1971, drunken warders roused prisoners at 1 a.m., made them strip naked and endure a rough three-hour search during which 28 prisoners were seriously injured, including ANC leader Govan Mbeki and SWAPO leader Herman Toivo ja Toivo. The search was mainly directed against the Namibian prisoners, who arrived on Robben Island from 1967 as their war for independence intensified.

Then, in 1973, Justice Minister Jimmy Kruger visited the Island and met with Nelson Mandela and a group led by Mac Maharaj. Afterward, Maharaj recalled, those who met with Kruger felt he had come 'on a kite-flying mission to find out whether there was scope among political prisoners for a negotiating base with separate development as the underlying principle'. He was turned down flat. It would take a decade before tentative steps were made again. The next occasion came when then Law and Order Minister Louis le Grange visited Nelson Mandela and appointed Brigadier Aucamp to act as a go-between with the ANC and Pretoria. Sometimes, Prison Board officials called prisoners before them and asked political questions, but Mandela instructed his fellow prisoners to limit their answers only to prison conditions and say 'send your political representatives to talk with our political leaders, don't talk to me'.

Meanwhile, on the mainland, workers in Durban had staged an illegal march (black people were neither allowed to march or belong to unions) demanding a 1c increase in wages. It was the seed of the trade union movement. By 1977, a handwritten 27-page document – which, if typed, would amount to some 100 pages – circulated on the Island. It can confidently be said that this was the blueprint for the organised labour movement that was slowly being developed. Entitled *Labour Organisation in Our Revolution* (*see* page 112), it was a brilliant treatise on the need for entrenching a working-class struggle, and contained an easy to follow, step by step manual for organising and running a union.

PRISON CONDITIONS

By 1977, after the Soweto uprising of June 16, 1976, the jails were full. Young people were fleeing across South Africa's borders to join the ANC or PAC, and townships had developed an unease that was to last for almost two decades.

In February 1977, Amnesty International complained to Justice Minister Jimmy Kruger that it had received complaints about assaults against 35 Black Consciousness prisoners working in the lime quarry on the Island when dogs were released on them. Kruger ignored the complaint, but nine Robben Island prisoners – including people like Saths Cooper, Muntu Myeza, Aubrey Makoape, Rudolf Knight and others – took the prison to court. The court ruled that prisoners could refuse to work in dangerous conditions.

Cooper's luck continued. During a search of his cell, warders found a radio hidden in an air vent but laid no charges, because they would have had to reveal the name of their informer, Daluxolo Luthuli. A former ANC cadre who left South Africa when he was 15 and fought in important battles with the ANC in Zimbabwe, Luthuli returned to South Africa and became part of the police death squads, an askari and later an Inkatha warlord – all of which he admitted almost two decades later to the Truth and Reconciliation Commission hearings.

By May 1977, ongoing publicity about poor prison conditions led to the prison authorities taking a carefully selected group of 25 journalists – all

THE MOST POPULAR RECORDS ON THE CAMPUS

OUR OWN "TOP 20": "WITH VOTES."

1. ELLA AND BASIE. ———— 12.

2. BACK TO BACK. — ———— 11.

3 BROOK BENTON TODAY. —— 8.

4 JOE WILLIAMS —— 8.

5 OUR KIND OF JAZZ —— 8

6. LIE TO ME —— 7.

7. DARK CITY SISTERS —— 7.

8 BIG 18 —— 7.

9 BOOMSTRAAT. —— 7.

10 JOE LOSS PLAYS GLENN MILLER — 6.

11 A TOUCH OF LATIN — 6.

12. BEST OF ARGO JAZZ — 5.

13. COME CLOSER TO ME — 5

14. SESSION AT THE RIVERSIDE - 5.

15. MILES DAVIS. — 5

16. SIKHALO TWO. — 5

17. JULIE LONDON. — 4.

18. PORTRAIT OF NAT KING COLE. — 4

19. MEMPHIS UNDERGROUND. — 4.

20. JUST JAZZ — 4.

DIG THEM FOLKS!!! REAL COOL!!!

THE PRC. COMMITTEE

16'8'73

P.J. Silwane

Secretary - S.C.C.

Jazz was clearly the music political prisoners most enjoyed in the early 1970s.

vetted by the security police – on a one-time-only tour of the Island. Their articles were submitted for censorship and approval before publication. Govan Mbeki answered questions, but Walter Sisulu and Nelson Mandela, who were digging next to Herman Toivo ja Toivo, all refused to speak. General Roux explained that the Rivonia trialists and SWAPO prisoners were different from criminal prisoners: 'There is very little chance of their rehabilitation. They really believe in the things for which they have been sent to prison.'

At the time, there were 369 prisoners on the Island, only 13 of whom had had beds – which had to be prescribed by doctors. The lights in their cells burned 24 hours a day.

Nelson Mandela, prisoner 466/64, had about 40 books on his shelves, including the Bible, an economic history of Europe, an English dictionary and *The Naked Society* by Vance Packard. He had Vitamin C tablets and a box of soap powder. He exercised regularly and, in the decade to April 1977, his weight increased only 500 grams to 78 kilograms. He had a small desk, a chair, a tiny wall cupboard and a bed. On his desk were photographs of a buxom tribal dancer and a young, beautiful Winnie in a beaded headdress. A row of green tomatoes lay ripening in front of her photograph.

The tomatoes were from Elias Motsoaledi, a fellow Rivonia trialist who died a few years after his release in 1989. From the first days of his incarceration, he cultivated a garden in the dry white soil of Robben Island. From pips, he planted what became a flourishing grape arbour, two peach trees and tomato plants, as well as marigolds and other flowers. One day, a glum Kathrada returned to his cell after having been subjected to disciplinary action, to find that Motsoaledi had left a precious bunch of grapes and two juicy peaches on his table. It was his first taste of those fruits in 12 years.

Two months after the media visit, the Rivonia trialists were promoted to prison category group A and were allowed to buy coffee, peanut butter, margarine and apricot jam from the prison store. Purchases could not exceed R8 a month. They could now receive two visits a month and receive three letters or two additional letters in lieu of visits. And they could keep photo albums.

Prison regulations eased again in January 1978, when warders began taping the morning and evening radio news bulletins and the SABC news magazine 'Radio Today'. After careful censorship (even from what was then the propaganda arm of the government), at 6 p.m. each day the prison would fall silent while all ears turned to the censored news. This of course fuelled intellectual debate and gave prisoners a clearer idea of what was happening on the mainland.

But apartheid paranoia was intensifying. Arden Bosman, who was 14 when he was incarcerated on the Island – because police suspected he was in contact with exiles at his school in Lesotho – was politically naïve. It had cost his impoverished mother all her savings to send him to Lesotho, away from the turbulence of Noordgesig, a coloured area bordering on Soweto, but on his return for school holidays he was arrested as a 'terrorist subversive'. Arden was terrified of jail, but soon found a core of young people of similar age he could safely mingle with. In that year, on June 9, 1978, Kruger admitted to Parliament that six children under the age of 16 were being held on the Island, after being found guilty of sabotage. One, he said, was 14 years old and five others were a year older.

Prisoners contributed according to their means towards recreational equipment.

1/3/77	DONATIONS – TENNIS BALLS		THANK YOU
NO.	NAME	AMOUNT	SIGNATURE
864/64	E. J. DANIELS	R 6,00	E. J. Daniels
2/75	KADER HASSIM	R 6,00	Kader Hassim
8/65	L. CHIBA	R 6,00	Chiba
69/64	B. NAIR R3,00		Nair
130/67	M. K. Dingake	R 5.00	M. K. Dingake
A14/71	J. E. APRIL	R 2.00	J. E. April
107/67	J. N. Pokela	R 1.00	Pokela
67/64	A. Mlangeni	R 1,00	Mlangeni
182/72	R. WILCOX	R 4.00	Wilcox
595/65	J. FUZILE	R 1-00	J. M. Fuzile
5/74	T. T. CHOLO	R 1, 00	Cholo
21/65	T. H. JA-TOIVO	R 3.00	T. Toivo
466/64	N. R. Mandela	R 5.00	N. R. Mandela
20/67	Wilton J. Mkwayi	R 1,00	W. Z. Mkwayi
470/64	R. M. Mhlaba	R 2,00	Mhlaba
183/72	S. R. Venkatrathnam	R 5-00	Venkatrathnam
1/75	J. B. Tuani	R 2.00	
468/64	A. M. Kathrada	R 2-00	Am Kathrada
190/72	F. ANTHONY	R 5-00	F. Anthony

GEVANGENIS
ONTVANGSKANTOOR
RECEPTION OFFICE
15 -3- 1977
PRIVAATSAK/PRIVATE BAG
ROBBENEILAND/ROBBEN ISLAND
PRISON

MAYIBUYE CENTRE

THE 1980s:
HOW DO WE RELEASE THEM?

*The passions which a revolution has roused do not disappear at its
close. A sense of instability remains in the midst of re-established
order ... desires still remain extremely enlarged, while the means of
satisfying them are diminished by the day ...*
ALEXIS DE TOCQUEVILLE, DEMOCRACY IN AMERICA, 1848.

L
ike the 1950s, the 1980s represented a turning point for South Africa.
During the 1980s, four states of emergency clamped the land in terror.
Prisons were full – with 40% of those incarcerated being children under the age
of 18 – death squads emerged, people disapeared and torture became the
norm, as did the bugging of telephones, tampering of mail, and secret graves
of executed freedom fighters. The words of French novelist Albert Camus,
written in an underground Resistance newspaper in 1943, could have been
written about South Africa in the terrifying, dying years of apartheid. Camus
wrote: 'It is a great deal to face torture and death when you know that hatred
and violence are empty things in themselves ... We paid for it with humilations
and silences, with bitter experiences, with prison sentences, with executions at
dawn, with desertions and separations, with daily pangs of hunger, with ema-
ciated children and above all with humiliation of our human dignity.

'It took us all that time to find out if we had the right to kill men, if we
were allowed to add to the frightful misery of this world. And because of that
time lost and recaptured, our defeat accepted and surmounted, those scruples
paid for with blood, we French have the right to think today that we entered
this war with hands clean ... with a great victory won against injustice.'

During the 1980s weekends were spent going to funerals of activists, many
of whom died during protests or in police custody. The funerals often led to
tense confrontations between the police and mourners, with tear gas, shooting
and more deaths. At wakes, young people would toyi-toyi in tight circles, red
dust rising from their feet, and sing about watering the tree of liberation with
their blood.

The tree drank deep.

Ronnie Mamoepa was a skinny kid who knew the slogans and songs by
heart, and could raise his knees higher than most in the toyi-toyi. He was four
years old when the Rivonia trialists were incarcerated. By the 1980s, there had
not been a year since he was 14 that he had not been detained in police cells
for days, weeks or months at a time. At the age of 18, on 12 March 1980, he

was convicted of terrorism (the first time he had ever been charged) with eight others – the Atteridgeville Nine. Two of his co-accused, unionist Jerry Majatladi and journalist Thami Makhwanazi, received seven-year sentences. The remainder received five years each. They were found guilty of recruiting young people for military training by the ANC and for conspiring to over-throw the state.

Before they were transferred to Robben Island, the Atteridgeville Nine were held at Leeuwkop Prison north of Johannesburg, fringing the city's wealthiest suburbs. Outwardly idyllic, with cows grazing in lush pastures around tiered dams dotted with ducks and geese, Mamoepa said their cells were so narrow it was impossible to stretch out one's arms. There were buck-ets instead of toilets and, at weekends, warders would place laxatives in their food and lock them up for 23 hours. On a bitterly cold morning in May, the prisoners were transferred from Leeuwkop. They were given canvas jackets and cardboard boxes filled with bread. Twenty prisoners set off at 3 a.m. in a prison truck equipped with a toilet that flushed onto the road. Arriving in Cape

A relative of one of the common prisoners shows off the gift made for him by the prisoner.

GEORGE HALLETT

Town, they were taken to Quay Five. Warders with dogs and guns lined the jetty. They yelled in Afrikaans: 'Tutu, look straight ahead.' (At that time, Desmond Tutu was the Anglican Dean of Johannesburg. Though hated by many whites for his outspoken stance against injustice, he would later be awarded the Nobel Peace Prize.)

Ronnie recalls: 'When we arrived on the Island it was the first time I met Africans who spoke Xhosa, I spoke Sotho and assumed all black people did. We could not understand each other. The warders told us to squat and shut up and cut our hair. They removed our belts and shoes and told us, "julle is nou bandi-ete"' (you are now bandits).

'We washed ourselves with a liquid soap used in factories, we mixed hair shampoo with it to get foam, otherwise the seawater would prevent foam. Our bodies felt so dry after being washed. We all still have a skin rash from the Island. The Island lives with you.'

Ronnie was placed in Section C, and then in Section E with people like Dan Montsisi and Murphy Morobe. 'Each day at about 3 p.m. we would get medicine bottles and fill them in the kitchen with boiling water. Before closing the bottle, we would seal it with plastic, then wrap it in a raincoat and a blanket so we could have tea at night.

'We would buy everything communally. Whether you had money or not, you had access to things, so an elite could not form in a cell. Every cell contained about 33 people and in each section there were four cells.'

Ronnie was a painter: 'Every section was separate but no decision could be made until all sections had agreed to it, and painters were among the only people who could move with information between all sections.'

Censorship of the cherished few letters allowed each year was harsh. 'Sometimes you would get a letter with just the address, the greeting and closure, the rest had been cut by censors. All communication had to be in English. As we conversed with visitors we could hear tapes rolling.'

On October 1, 1980, Nelson Mandela brought an application before the Supreme Court to prevent prison warders from listening to conversations between prisoners and lawyers. Judge President H. E. P. Watermeyer and Justice E. M. Grosskopf – whose son Hein would later outrage the white Afrikaner community by becoming an ANC soldier – reserved judgement.

WINDS OF CHANGE

Outside prison the momentum for change was growing. A Johannesburg newspaper survey found that 54% of whites would support Mandela's release. In jail, prisoners were now allowed to play tennis; Mandela reportedly had a 'mean backhand'. The most popular sport was soccer, but most prisons had facilities too for athletics, volleyball, table tennis and softball. Newspapers were now allowed, with the *Rand Daily Mail* being the most coveted.

Life on the Island was relatively slow and settled; camraderie had developed with the rebels of 1976, and there was time for laughter. Although Rivonia trialist Andrew Mlangeni wryly reported that it was a 'great disadvantage that Mandela, Mbeki and Mhlaba were mission educated. In lighter moments you wanted to crack blue jokes and they wouldn't allow it. The worst Mbeki could say was, "you swine". Mandela couldn't even say that. Once Mhlaba was really angry and he said, "you, you … " and finally said "you fascist": It was the worst insult he could think of.'

Other events also led to humour. Because of the cold and dust from the lime quarries, Indres Naidoo had a perpetually running nose. One day, in a fit of spite, a warder confiscated his handkerchief. After weeks of protest by prisoners, the authorities finally gave each one a small square of red cloth to use. However, Indres recalls, the daily sight of rows of little red squares of cloth blowing in the wind as they dried angered the authorities, who accused prisoners of flying the red flag. The cloths were confiscated and replaced by soft squares of khaki-coloured cloth.

The ANC in exile had, meanwhile, stepped up its guerilla campaign, and South African security forces under President Pieter W. Botha struck back with cross-border raids, destabilisation of neighbouring states and death squads At the same time the government still hoped to release cowed ANC leaders, or at least to foster disunity among the liberation movements. In March 1982, the government introduced the Prisons Amendment Bill, which allowed for remission of sentences for certain categories of prisoners. Justice Minister Kobie Coetsee said government would consider releasing political prisoners. His comments excited the attention of the press when, the following month, Nelson Mandela, Walter Sisulu, Ahmed Kathrada, Raymond Mhlaba and Andrew Mlangeni were abruptly moved from Robben Island to Pollsmoor Prison in Cape Town.

In July 1982, the government announced the release of seven political prisoners, but would not name them. Investigations by the *Rand Daily Mail* ascertained the seven had been jailed under the Suppression of Communism Act and had negligible time left to serve. Henry Africa (25) of Johannesburg, as an example, had a month left of a four-month sentence.

New 'plans' for the Island surfaced, with the government saying that it was considering converting the facility into Defence Force base, once the prisoners had been moved out. In February 1983, the government announced there were 286 prisoners on Robben Island serving sentences for crimes committed against the state, of whom 40 were serving life sentences.

Shifting from its long-standing policy against attacking civilian targets, the ANC now began guerilla attacks in the knowledge that civilian losses could occur. Land mines were placed on roads used by the military in the rural northern Transvaal – attacks which exacted a civilian toll. Then, in May 1983, the ANC placed itself firmly at the front of the public mind when it detonated a car bomb outside Air Force headquarters in Pretoria, killing 19 and injuring 215. White panic reached new levels, but already the ANC was restrategising.

In January of that year, the Dutch Reformed minister Alan Boesak had told a meeting of longtime ANC ally, the Transvaal Indian Congress, in Johannesburg, that a united democratic front was needed to fight apartheid. By August, the United Democratic Front (UDF) was launched. The UDF embraced 600 organisations opposed to apartheid. It played a critical role in unifying resistance and paving the way for the release of political prisoners, the unbanning of organisations and negotiations – but not without a high toll in human life and suffering, and many more inmates for Robben Island and other prisons.

The UDF campaigned against the tricameral parliament introduced on September 3, 1984. This superficial inclusion of coloured and Indian people with small constituencies was intended to give a semblance of power-sharing. On September 3, riots that would last for months broke out in the Vaal townships near Johannesburg. It was an omen of what was to come. While international pressure intensified for Mandela's release – with 4 000 prominent international celebrities signing a petition – South Africa applied pressure of its own to neighbouring states.

By June 1984, Foreign Minister Pik Botha and Defence Minister Magnus Malan met top officials of Angola's MPLA government in Lusaka and demanded that they close ANC camps in the country. Many camps were already heavily infiltrated by South African agents who poisoned water or assassinated key figures, causing intense paranoia in ANC exile circles. In the same year, President Samora Machel of Mozambique was pressured into signing the Nkomati Accord, under the terms of which he ordered ANC cadres out of Mozambique. The Swazi government followed suit.

LEADERSHIP IN WAITING

As these events unfolded, liberal politician Helen Suzman visited Mandela and his cohorts at Pollsmoor Prison and found that they had less facilities than on the Island. The ANC leadership on the Island was able to maintain clandestine contact with those in Pollsmoor and in exile; lawyers were often primary conduits of information.

The 1980s sometimes brought unexpected sources of joy. Most prisoners missed children – more, Neville Alexander said, than women. At Eid (a Muslim festival) in 1983 a lawyer visited Ahmed Kathrada with his two-year-old daughter, who stubbornly refused to remain outside the meeting room (children were not allowed to see prisoners). A guard relented, and Kathrada recalled, 'it was the first time I had come close to a child in 20 years, I hugged and kissed her. I went back to the cell with my mind in a whirl, it took me some time to relax and adjust after having seen this child. Fortunately a few years later they allowed children to visit us.'

In November, 1984, Mandela was separated from other prisoners. He recalls: 'I thought I should approach government and ask for a meeting between them and the ANC. I agonised that I would approach government without consulting with my colleagues, but I felt that if I did they would reject my move because of our hatred of National Party politicians.

'I felt the time was right for negotiations', a sense he acquired from visiting politicians, judges and top prison officials. 'I approached government and had discussions with Kobie Coetsee who said talks must be secret. I said confidential, yes, but secret, no. I wanted to see my four comrades in Pollsmoor. The authorities said I could see them one by one, so I called comrade Walter Sisulu. I calculated that if I convinced him, he would help me convince the rest. He was very diplomatic and said "Madiba, I have nothing against negotiations, but would prefer that they start first, not us." I said "Comrade Tshepo (hope) if you are not against negotiations, it doesn't matter who starts."

'I called comrade Raymond Mhlaba, who said, "what were you waiting for all this time, you should have done this long ago". Comrade Kathrada disagreed. Comrade Mlangeni agreed. I smuggled a letter to the leadership outside. A reply came from Oliver Tambo, who was my law partner from 1942 to 1960, a very clever, efficient fellow with impressive vision. In his reply there was disapproval. He said, "what are you discussing with these fellows?" I answered in one line, "I am discussing the ANC and government meeting".

Later in a memo I explained I was discussing violence, negotiations, the alliance with the SA Communist Party and majority rule. The ANC agreed.' Mandela then began briefing political leaders from around the country.

'Government appointed a top team of negotiators: General Willemse (head of prisons), Coetsee, Neil Barnard (head of the National Intelligence Service), Fanie van der Merwe (constitutional expert) and Mike Louw of NIS. Then I saw PW (Botha) in 1989. He received me very well.' Mandela was moved from Pollsmoor to a cottage in the grounds of Victor Verster prison near Paarl. But the security forces were still acting ruthlessly against the people. Townships were battlefields, and there was no indication outside very select, secret circles that negotiations were taking place.

THE TURNING POINT

The final document submitted to political education classes at Robben Island on July 31, 1990, by the Island's Central Political Committee reflected that, from 1984 to 1985, 'we saw the remarkable increase of MK activities in our country. (This) coupled with the militant mass uprisings of our people forced the enemy to declare a state of emergency for four consecutive years. These repressives measures failed to crush or silence democratic forces. We saw the emergence of strong organisations, e.g. Cosatu, SA Youth Congress and National Education Co-Ordinating Committee. Apartheid served as a fetter to economic development with sanctions and disinvestment.

'A turning point was the defeat of the SADF at Cuito Cuanavale (fought in Angola in 1987). This forced the regime to concede to the implementation of UN Resolution 435. SA gained a lot of goodwill internationally by negotiating the independence of Namibia. The imperialists realised, particularly America and Britain, that if the SA regime were to embark on negotiations it could signal the end of SA isolation. Our organisation succesfully rallied the Frontline States (neighbouring southern African countries) and the rest of the world to accept its position (the Harare Declaration) on negotiations.

'The regime realised it could no more rely on repressive measures to stop our peoples march to freedom. We saw the release of our leaders, the Rivonia trialists, the allowing of marches and protests. But government's main objectives were to break out of isolation, ensure economic growth and more profits for capitalists, to demobilise our people and weaken democratic forces.' The document admitted ANC shortcomings: 'at grassroots level our people organisations are relatively weak ... there's a lack of dynamic contact between the leadership, membership and the masses at large.'

By the late 1980s, apartheid, even without sanctions, was bankrupting the fiscus. As far back as 1979, Botha had tried to win disgruntled capitalists to his side, with some success. He kept warning that the ANC was a radical group manipulated by communists. But by September 1985, with the townships at war, and detentions running into the tens of thousands, big business decided to see the ANC. Gavin Relly and Zach de Beer, the heads of South Africa's major corporation Anglo American, together with liberal businessman Tony Bloom of Premier Milling, met with the ANC. At the same time, Harry Oppenheimer – South Africa's wealthiest man – publicly backed the release of Nelson Mandela.

So many business people and academics visited Lusaka to meet with the ANC that Deputy Foreign Minister Ron Miller said in November 1985 that the government would withdraw the passports of anyone who visited the ANC in Lusaka. So meetings took place in Geneva, Paris and Dakar, Senegal. The government said it would release political prisoners if they renounced violence, while the ANC retorted that government had to renounce violence, too.

On Robben Island, the late 1980s brought improvements in prison conditions. By 1986, prisoners were allowed radios, but not shortwave receivers. They could own musical instruments and watch television and videos. A firm TV favourite was Bill Cosby. The prisoners were allowed to write poetry, and notebooks were soon crammed with poems – most of them not very good – about love, longing and revolution. They were prohibited from writing books, but some, like Govan Mbeki, had for years kept diaries that would become manuscripts. They were allowed hobbies and pets. All visits to political prisoners at Pollsmoor and Robben Island became contact visits. For most prisoners, the opportunity to touch a beloved after so many years was overwhelming.

Xolani Yengeni, a 17-year-old political activist, arrived into this relatively carefree atmosphere from the turbulence of the Eastern Cape townships in 1986. Sentenced for incitement, public violence and subversion as a result of school boycotts in Port Elizabeth, where he was a Congress of South African Students (COSAS) organiser, Xolani was detained with 15 others, of whom nine were charged. He was the only one convicted; the other eight managed to skip the country while on bail, which he was denied.

Xolani served four years on Robben Island. 'The relationship between inmates was very good, but the attitude of some warders was not. Most of us when we went to Robben Island had been detained and tortured and were bitter.' Before he was sent to Robben Island he was jailed at St Albans, a Port Elizabeth prison. He says conditions there were very bad. 'At 5 a.m. they would wake prisoners. We had to make our beds and wash before 6 a.m. when they would have inspection. There were only two showers for 20 people and if you weren't fast enough by the time you got to the shower it was cold.'

In his soft, gentle voice he says: 'They put me in a cell with gangsters. I was 17 years old and some harassed me. If you were a young boy the boers (warders) would say, this is a meisie (girl) you must naai him (have sex with him). I had a friend there, Mzwandele, who was 19, a COSAS member, he died in prison for resisting those conditions. He was beaten to death by the boers, who told prisoners that a qabani (comrade) had hanged himself.

'I slept with a plate against my heart because you never knew when these gangsters would attack. If a young boy refused their sexual advances they would wait until 8 p.m. when the lights were switched off, then go into a corner and caucus and go to anyone and stab you to death.' Arriving at Robben Island, he found that conditions were safer, but 'there was no sense that negotiations were going on, people were talking about saving the country by force. But developments in eastern Europe, the coming of Gorbachev, and Cuba leaving Angola, made us realise military change would not be possible.'

It was a realisation that Mandela and the ANC had also reached. In July 1987, the Institute for Democratic Alternatives – headed by Dr Frederick van Zyl Slabbert and Alex Boraine – led a large group of top businessmen, academics, writers and poets to Dakar for talks with ANC leaders, including Thabo Mbeki. The ANC put forward the notion of a two-sided negotation process, with the government and its partners on one side and the collective and allied 'forces of freedom' on the other.

On August 13, 1987, P. W. Botha told prison officials to prepare the release of 77-year-old Rivonia trialist Govan Mbeki. Nonetheless, government death squads intensified their grisly work at home and abroad: in the first four months of 1988, attacks had been perpetrated against eight prominent ANC exiles. Dulcie September was shot dead in Paris, while Albie Sachs had his arm blown off in Maputo.

This did not deter the ANC. In May 1988, it released a draft constitution for South Africa. The government funded black puppet organisations and negotiated with them. Fredrick W. de Klerk, a cabinet minister and Transvaal

---

In February 1995 more than 1 000 ex-political prisoners gathered together again on Robben Island for a historic and symbolic reunion.

MAYIBUYE CENTRE

leader of the National Party, built up ties with moderate black leaders with their own constituencies, such as Inkatha's Mangosuthu Buthelezi and Labour Party leader Alan Hendrickse. Voted into power in September 1989, De Klerk released the remaining Rivonia trialists a month later, with the exception of Mandela, who was released on February 11 the following year.

As political prisoners sensed that their release might be imminent, many either withdrew psychologically or became aggressive. Cape Town health professionals issued a press statement on January 25, 1990, calling for pre-release counselling: 'We are appalled that the government continues to release political prisoners with little or no advance warning to them, their families or their organisations. In the past month alone, nearly 40 political prisoners have been released, some with as little as 15 minutes advance warning to pack their belongings, say goodbye to fellow prisoners and prepare themselves emotionally for their release. This is causing a great deal of emotional distress and ill feeling among those released and those left behind bars.'

Release carried its own trauma, as prisoners manifested physical symptoms including headaches, psychomatic illnesses, stomach disorders, increased irritability, short temper and anxiety attacks. They were released into another country, one no longer the same as when they had left it 20, 15, 10 or even 5 years before. Some could not find their families or their homes and, penniless, turned to alcohol or suicide.

Some prisoners from Robben Island never made it home. They had contracted HIV on the Island and by 1987 prison authorities began moving the first HIV-infected prisoners to Pollsmoor Prison, where they could get better medical care before dying of AIDS-related illnesses in the prison hospital or nearby clinics. They included a number of well-known ANC activists. To this day, the cause of their illnesses and deaths remains an unspoken secret in a nation still in denial about an AIDS epidemic that by 2000 was seeing one in four South Africans infected and a rate of 1 800 new infections each day.

FREE AT LAST

Members of the MDM (Mass Democratic Movement; the succesor to the UDF) maintained constant contact with Mandela and with the ANC in exile. Newspapers were freely quoting the ANC's Lusaka spokesperson, Tom Sebina. National Union of Mineworkers secretary-general Cyril Ramaphosa was a key figure in pre-release talks. On February 2, 1990, the ANC, PAC and other banned organisations had their restrictions lifted. Spontaneous parties took place all over the country and homemade ANC flags – in the party's colours of black, yellow and green – proliferated.

Shosholoza – work together. Prisoners sang as they heaved stone in the quarries and again for this reunion with the media press.

The following week, Ramaphosa was admitted with pneumonia to the Rand Clinic in Johannesburg. He insisted on a telephone at his bedside. A chartered aircraft was on 24-hour standby to take him, Mohammed Valli Moosa and other MDM leaders to Cape Town the minute government told them Mandela's release was imminent. Ramaphosa was reading historian Barbara Tuchman's *The March of Folly* when the phone rang. Removing his drip he checked out of hospital and headed for Cape Town.

The next day, after an interminable television broadcast, a convoy of cars stopped at the gates of Victor Verster Prison, where crowds waited. Hand-in-hand Mandela and his wife Winnie stepped out of the vehicle and walked through the gates to freedom. Champagne corks popped in newspaper offices; out on the streets a cacophony of car horns rose above a sleepy Sunday afternoon; church bells rang; and thousands of people took to the streets laughing, singing, cheering, chanting. His freedom was the symbolic liberation of all South Africans, black and white.

In *The March of Folly* (1984), Barbara Tuchman wrote: 'To abandon a policy that is turning sour is more laudable than ignominious, if the change is genuine and carried out purposefully.' Perhaps F. W. de Klerk never envisioned that change would become unstoppable, yet it is hard to imagine how he could have believed it would not be. Therefore history will salute him before it condemns him. Tuchman also noted that 'Large minds are needed for magnanimity.' Although she was writing of events in America between 1772 and 1775, she might almost have been describing Nelson Mandela. From the beginning, Mandela displayed this sympathy toward his gravest foes. His actions are similar to those of Solon, chief magistrate of Athens in 6th century B.C., whose fairness and justness as a statesman caused Barbara Tuchman to comment: 'An absence of overriding personal ambition together with shrewd common sense are among the essential components of wisdom'.

THE PRESENT

'Everything that happens in this world happens at the time God chooses. He sets the time for ... killing and the time for healing, the time for tearing down and the time for building, the time for sorrow and the time for joy.'

ECCLESIASTES 3

The last prisoners and warders left Robben Island in December 1996; for many of the warders, some of whom had lived on the windy knoll for as long as three decades, it was a sad farewell. Their departure followed a decision by the South African government, on September 4 of that year, that the Island should become a world Heritage Site. In January 1997 it was declared a Cultural Institution.

It was at this time that Professor André Odendaal, of the then Mayibuye Centre, began living on the Island with a few key maintenance staff to begin developing the Robben Island Museum, the Sobukwe house and other facets of the Robben Island heritage site. The Centre was originally established at the University of the Western Cape with files, photographs, artefacts and documents from the International Defence and Aid Fund, which supported political prisoners for more than three decades from London, and assiduously collected the minutiae that documented South Africa's apartheid years and the stories of those opposed to apartheid. The Centre – now called the UWC-Robben Island Mayibuye Archives – brought the heart of Robben Island and political prisoner experience back to the Island.

Designed to serve a multiplicity of purposes, the Robben Island Museum emphasises the educational, ecological, tourism and conservation aspects of the Island. It was declared a world Heritage site by UNESCO in 1999, and is also a National Monument and a National Museum. Tours to Robben Island leave from the Nelson Mandela Gateway, which was opened by the former President himself in 2001, and forms part of the Victoria & Alfred Waterfront's Clock Tower Precinct. The Gateway building includes a Robben Island Museum shop, restaurant, and 150-seater auditorium, as well as exhibition areas, offices, boardrooms, and interactive, digital exhibits about the history of the Island and of South Africa under apartheid. The Gateway, a memorial representing the importance of the Island for South Africa's young democracy, leads out to a floating jetty, where visitors can board the ferries, bound for the Island.

BIBLIOGRAPHY AND INTERVIEWS

This book, though the widest ranging account yet of the Island, is by no means complete. I have included the names of libraries or resource centres where applicable. More needs to be researched in the future, and some of the clues to where information can be found are contained in this bibliography.

RESEARCH SOURCES
SL: The Strange Library, Africana Museum, Johannesburg
SAMM: The SA Military Museum, Saxonwold, Johannesburg
JPL: Johannesburg Public Library
JRL: Johannesburg Reference Library
MC: Mayibuye Centre, University of the Western Cape, Bellville, Cape Town
SAL: SA Library, Queen Victoria Street, Cape Town
SANA: SA National Archives, Roeland Street, Cape Town
TML: Times Media Library, Johannesburg
TCC: Collection Tim Couzens, Johannesburg

INTERVIEWS AND SPEECHES
Arden Bosman, Johannesburg, March 25, 1994.
W/O Magdalena Cillie, prison warder and wife of warder, Robben Island, December 6, 1993.
Dr Saths Cooper, Johannesburg, December 20, 1993.
Jean de la Harpe, Johannesburg, December 13, 1993.
Zane Erasmus, regional head, Cape Peninsula, Cape Nature Conservation Department, Milnerton, Cape Town, December 10, 1993.
Barry Feinberg, formerly of International Defence and Aid Fund, London, and latterly of Mayibuye Centre, University of the Western Cape; numerous discussions with since 1991.
Professor Jakes Gerwel, University of the Western Cape, speech at *Esiquithini Robben Island* exhibition. (MC)
Afrika Hlapo, ex-Robben Island prisoner, Bellville, Cape Town, December 7, 1993.
Ahmed Kathrada, 1993 (telephonic interview); speech at opening of *Esiquithini Robben Island* exhibition, SA Museum, Cape Town, 26 May 1993. (MC); transcript interview 26 May, 1993 with **Barry Feinberg** of Mayibuye Centre. (MC)

Correne Kemp, Parow, Cape Town, December 9, 1993.
Ronnie Mamoepa, Johannesburg, November 10, 1993, and various discussions thereafter.
Johnson Mlambo, PAC first deputy president, Johannesburg, October 25, 1993 and November 5, 1993, and associated discussions thereafter.
Wilton Mkwayi, August 3 and August 4 and December 13, 1994, and sundry discussions afterward.
Eric Molobi, Johannesburg, March 31, 1994.
Dr Johan Neethling, Department Nature Conservation, Cape Provincial Administration and chairman of Robben Island Advisory Committee, Cape Town, December 3 and December 7, 1993 and assorted chats thereafter.
Mayibuye Centre interview: **Professor André Odendaal** with **Barry Feinberg**, 10 June 1993.
Dullah Omar, Pretoria, 20 July 1994.
Bridgette Oppenheimer, Brenthurst, Johannesburg, November 18, 1993.
Walter Sisulu, 1993; various interviews.
Christmas Tinto, ANC executive member, Woodstock, Cape Town, December 2, 1993.
Desiree van Zyl, Robben Island storekeeper and wife of warder, Robben Island, December 10, 1993.
Dr Bruno Werz, Department of Marine Archaeology, University of Cape Town, Cape Town, November 30, 1993 and subsequent chats.
Norman Yengeni, 10 June 1990 (transcript of interview with Barry Feinberg). (MC)
Xolani Yengeni, Cape Town, 7 and 8 April, 1994.

Nelson Mandela's visit to Robben Island with **Andrew Mlangeni, Ahmed Kathrada** and other former prisoners with press corps, 11 February 1994.

Guided visit Robben Island, December 6, 1993 with **Sergeant Wayne Cook**, and informal – and unsanctioned – discussions with **prisoners**.

Numerous brief interviews and chats over the years with former Robben Island prisoners, their visitors and friends, including **Jerry Majatladi, Govan Mbeki, Tokyo Sexwale, Jacob Zuma, Elias Motsoaledi, Helen Joseph, Kgalema Motlanthe, Jean de la Harpe, Andrew Mapheto and others.**

TRAVELLER'S ACCOUNTS AND OTHER PRIMARY SOURCES

Assorted notes, menus, invoices, invitations, videos and other memorabilia from Desiree van Zyl, Robben Island, 1994.

Cape of Good Hope: Correspondence with the governor, relative to the state of the Kafir tribes and to the recent outbreak on the Eastern Frontier, with papers presented to Parliament, March 20, 1851 and May 2, 1851. (JRL)

Collected correspondence and other papers, Eddie Daniels. (MC)

Collected documents of Ahmed Kathrada relating to his incarceration on Robben Island and in Pollsmoor prison. (MC) Letter to Helen Joseph (30.11.86) and letters to Zohra (21.12.76; 24.12.75; 21.6.75; 22.3.75; 21.6.75; 22.3.75; 25.12.76; 19.6.76; 15.5.76; 28.5.77, 25.6.77; 26.10.80; 25.8.79). (MC)

Collected documents relating to Robben Island prisoners and their writings with regard to education, sport, entertainment, miscellaneous and letters. (MC)

'Consciencism' by Mac Maharaj, Robben Island Notebook. (MC)

Correspondence 'Relative to the State of the Kafir tribes on the Eastern frontier of the Colony' February 1847. (JRL)

Correspondence re: 'The state of the Kafir tribes and the recent outbreak on the Eastern frontier of the Colony', Feb 3, 1853. (JRL)

Fish, James W. *Robben Island, an account of 34 years gospel work amongst lepers of SA* (John Ritchie). (SL)

Gresley, G.F. *The early history of Robben Island.* Reprinted from the Cape Illustrated Magazine, 1895. (SL)

Handwritten copy of Mandela document (South). (MC)

HLL, *Missionary Evenings at Home.* Thomas Nelson and Sons, London, 1866. (SAL)

Letter to Seddick Isaacs from Richard Ndxolo, 11.9.76. (MC)

Mayibuye Centre categorised boxes 44, 48, 49, 50, 72, 73, 79, 83.

Mbeki, Govan. Discussion document for Robben Island inmates on the formation of Umkhonto we Sizwe. (MC)

Mbeki, Govan. Unpublished foreword, 'How they came to be' from *Prison Writings. David Philip, Cape Town, 1991.* (MC)

Medical Somerset Hospital Colmed Committee and Infirmary Robben Island, 1855. (SANA)

The Old Robben Island Association, records of meetings, 1957. (SAL Ref 662, TCC)

Political Imprisonment Release and Mental Health: The Case for Pre-Release Counselling, the Liaison Committee for the Release of Political Prisoners in the Western Cape, January 25, 1991 and related documents. (MC)

Ration scale for black prisoners, Robben Island. (MC)

Reports on the Government and aid Hospitals and Reports of the Inspector of Asylums for 1896. (SANA)

Robben Island letter book, 1875 to 1879. (SANA)

Robben Island letter book, May 3, 1848 to March 15, 1853. (SANA)

Robben Island letter book number 61, Lunatic Asylum, 7 April 1879 to 29 August 1883. (SANA)

Robben Island discussion books: 1: *The Rectification Campaign of 1957 in Peoples China,* 31, 21, 33, 34 – B Kondile, 25 'Philosophical Notebook', Mpukame, handwritten and including copies of newspaper and magazine articles, speeches, books or chapters from books and treatises by prisoners on a variety of subjects. (MC)

Robben Island Notebooks, Laloo Chiba No. 27 and No. 33, 1979. (MC)

Labour Organisation in Our Revolution, 1977, Robben Island Notebook. (MC)

2A, *Why Must Communists Undertake to Cultivate Themselves,* Robben Island discussion book bound with glue on bandage. (MC)

Rogers, Woodes. *A cruising voyage around the world.* A. Bell and B. Lintot, London, 1712. (SAL)

Stavorinus, Jan Splinter *Voyages to the East Indies.* Vol.1. G.G. & J. Robinson, 1798. (SAL)

Terry, Edward. *A Voyage to East India.* J Wilkie, London, 1777. (SAL)

Thompson, George. *Travels and Adventures in Southern Africa.* 2 vols. Henry Colburn, London, 1827. (SAL)

BOOKS

Alexander, Neville. *Robben Island Dossier,* 1964.

Beeton, Irene. *The Robben Island I know.* (SAL MSB60, TCC)

Botha, C. Graham. *General History and Social Life of the Cape of Good Hope.* C Struik, Cape Town, 1962. (SAL)

Brain, Peter. *SA Radar in World War Two.* SSS Radar Book Group, Cape Town and Johannesburg, 1993. (SAMM)

Bunting, Brian. *The Rise of the South African Reich.* International Defence and Aid Fund for Southern Africa, London, 1986.

Cameron, Charlotte. *A woman's winter in Africa.* Stanley Paul & Co, London, 1913. (SAL)

Crawford, R. J. M., H. G. v.D. Boonstra, B. M. Dyer, and L. Upfold. *Recolonization of Robben Island by African Penguins 1893 – 1992.* Sea Fisheries Research Institute.

de Kock, Victor. *By Strength of Heart.* NV Drukkerij, Netherlands, 1953. (SAL)

de Villiers, Simon A. *Robben Island.* C. Struik, 1971. (Strange Library, Johannesburg).

Dingake, Michael. *My Fight Against Apartheid.* Kliptown Books, London, 1990.

Dlamini, Moses. *Moses Dlamini Prisoner No 872/64.* Penguin Books. (SAL)

Dlamini, Moses. *Robben Island, Hell-Hole, Reminiscences of a Political Prisoner.* Spokesman, Great Britain, 1984. (SAL)

Eagleheart, Clinton. *Eric of the Cape.* Hought & Scott-Snell, London, 1935. (SAL)

Green, Lawrence. *So few are free.* Howard Timmins, Cape Town, 1946. (SAL)

Green, Lawrence. *Strange Africa.* Howard Timmins, Cape Town (reprinted 1974).

Johns, Sheridan and R Hunt Davis, Jr. *The Struggle Against Apartheid 1948 – 1990* Oxford University Press, 1991.

Laidler, P. W. *The Growth and Government of Cape Town.* Unie-Volkspers, Cape Town, 1939. (SAL)

Laver, Margaret P. H., and others. *Sailor Women, Sea Women, Swans.* Swans Historical Fund, Simonstown, 1982. (SAMM)

Lewis, Ethelreda. *The Harp.* Hodder and Stoughton, circa 1927. (Personal collection, Tim Couzens Collection.)

Lodge, Tom. *Black Politics in South Africa since 1945.* Ravan Press, Johannesburg, 1983.

MacMillan, William Miller. *Bantu, Boer and Briton: The Making of the South African Native Problem.* Faber and Gwyer Limited, London, 1928.

Mandela, Nelson. *Long Walk to Freedom.* Macdonald Purnell, 1994.

Markovitz, Irving Leonard. *Power and Class in Africa.* Prentice Hall, New Jersey, 1977.

Mbeki, Govan. *South Africa: The Peasants' Revolt.* Penguin, Middlesex, 1964. (SAL)

Meer, Fatima. *Higher than Hope.* Institute for Black Research, Madiba Publishers, Durban, 1988.

Mostert, Noel. *Frontiers.* Pimlico. London, 1993.

Naidoo, Indres. *Prisoner 885/63, Island in Chains.* (As told to Albie Sachs.) Penguin Books, 1982. (SAL)

Newman, W. A. *Biographical memoir of John Montagu.* A.S. Robertson, Cape Town, 1855. (SAL)

Oberholster, J. J. *The Historical Monuments of SA.* Rembrandt van Rijn Foundation for Culture, 1972.

Orpen, Neil and H. F. Martin. *South Africa at War.* Purnell, 1979. (SAMM)

Pieres, J. B. *The Dead will Arise.* Ravan Press, Johannesburg, 1989.

Pudi, Ranko. *The illustrated life of Makhanda..* Skotaville Publishers, Johannesburg, 1984. (SAL)

Rodney, Walter. *How Europe Underdeveloped Africa.* Howard University Press, Washington, D.C., 1982

Schadeberg, Jurgen. (ed.) *Robben Island.* (to which the author contributed a chapter) 1994.

Sparks, Allister. *The Mind of South Africa.* William Heinemann, 1990.

Standard Encyclopaedia of Southern Africa. Volume 9, Nasou Limited, 1973.

Survey of Race Relations in SA. 1983, Volume 37, The Institute of Race Relations.

Suzman, Helen. *In No Uncertain Terms.* Jonathan Ball Publishers, Johannesburg 1993.

Theal, George McCall. *History of South Africa before 1795.* C. Struik, Cape Town, 1964. (JPL)

Werz, Dr Bruno. 'Maritiem argeologiese onder-soeke in 'n Suid-Afrikaanse konteks: doeis-telling, metode en praktyk', *Tydskrif vir Geesteswetenskappe*,1, Uitgegee deur Die Suid-Afrikaanse Akademie vir Wetenskap en Kuns, March, 1993.

Werz, Dr Bruno. 'The excavation of the Oosterland in Table Bay: the first systematic exercise in maritime archeology in southern Africa'. *Suid-Afrikaanse Tydskrif vir Wetenskap*, Vol 88, February 1992. 'Maritime Archeological Project Table Bay: Aspects of the first field season'. *SA Archeological Society Goodwin Series* 7:33 – 9, 1993.

Werz, Dr Bruno. 'Tafelbaai Gee Sy Geheime Prys: 'n Histories-Argeologiese ondersoek van die VOC-skip *Oosterland*'. Huegenot Society of SA, Bulletin 29, 1991–92.

Werz, Dr Bruno. 'Saving a Fragment of our Underwater Heritage', *Historical Society of Cape Town*, Vol 4, No 4, 1989.

Williams, Donovan. (ed.) *The Journal and Selected Writings of the Reverend Tiyo Soga*. A.A. Balkema, Cape Town, 1983. (SAL)

Zwelonke, D. M. *Robben Island*. Heinemann, 1973.

PERIODICALS AND MAGAZINES

Barron, Chris, 'My Famous Prisoner', *Sunday Times*, May 15, 1994.

Green, Pippa, 'No Man's Island', *Cosmopolitan* May, 1991.

Molo Songololo, Issue 82, 1993.

Rand Daily Mail, Sunday Times, The Star, The Sowetan, Sunday Tribune from 1961 to October, 1993 (TML); *Finance Week* archives 1983–94.

The New York Times, 19 October 1993.

Vogue (Paris), Dec/Jan 1994, guest edited by Nelson Mandela.

MISCELLANEOUS AND OTHER PUBLICATIONS

Cape Nature Conservation Department. *Island Reserves Master Plan*.

Cape Nature Conservation Department. *Report on the Large Mammals of Robben Island*. 8 November 1985.

Daniels, Eddie. *Robben Island: There and Back 1964 – 1979*. Unpublished manuscript. (MC)

Deacon, Janette. 'Protection of Historical Shipwrecks through the National Monuments Act' (speech) National Monuments Council, Cape Town, 25 March, 1993.

Depament of Correctional Services, Robben Island factsheet, 1993.

Department of Correctional Services, Robben Island brochure, 1993.

Erasmus, Zane. 'Some Comments on the Conservation Management of Robben Island', Cape Nature Conservation Department, September, 1993.

Hofmeyr, G.S. *King Williamstown and the Xhosa, 1854 to 1861*. Thesis for degree of Master of Arts in History at the University of Cape Town, 1981. (SAL)

Kozol, James. *Sir George Grey in South Africa, 1854 to 1861: His policies, schemes for federation and recall*. Unpublished thesis presented to the Department of History and the Faculty of the Graduate College, University of Nebraska, Omaha, USA, 1970. (SAL)

Letters to author from Andy Cockroft, Bruce Dyer, Rob Tarr Sea Fisheries Institute.

Mbeki, Govan. *The roots of the struggle for Liberation*. Chapter 8: 'The new option'. Unpubished manuscript. (MC)

Penn, Nigel, Harriet Deacon and Neville Alexander. *Robben Island. The politics of rock and sand*. University of Cape Town Department of Adult Education and Extra-Mural Studies, 1992.

Smith, Pam. *Robben Island, 1591–1920*. Dissertation, 1967. (SAL)

Werz, Dr Bruno. *Robben Island Shipwrecks, A Cultural Resource Management Exercise in the Underwater Environment*. Manuscript, 1993.

Werz, Dr Bruno and Janette Deacon. *Operation Sea Eagle: Final report on a survey of shipwrecks around Robben Island*. Department of Archaeology, University of Cape Town and National Monuments Council, Cape Town, July, 1992.

INDEX